A WAR
OF WORDS

A WAR OF WORDS

The Rhetorical Leadership of JEFFERSON DAVIS

R. JARROD ATCHISON

The University of Alabama Press
Tuscaloosa

The University of Alabama Press
Tuscaloosa, Alabama 35487-0380
uapress.ua.edu

Hardcover edition published 2017.
Paperback edition published 2019.
eBook edition published 2017.

Typeface: Sabon

Cover image: Jefferson Davis, three quarter length portrait, facing right, by photographer Mathew B. Brady, approximately 1823–1896; courtesy of the Library of Congress Prints and Photographs Division
Cover design: Todd Lape / Lape Designs

Paperback ISBN: 978-0-8173-5946-1

A previous edition of this book has been catalogued by the Library of Congress as follows:
Library of Congress Cataloging-in-Publication Data
Names: Atchison, R. Jarrod (Robert Jarrod), 1979–
Title: A war of words : the rhetorical leadership of Jefferson Davis / R. Jarrod Atchison.
Description: Tuscaloosa : The University of Alabama Press, [2017] | Includes bibliographical references and index.
Identifiers: LCCN 2016040699| ISBN 9780817319403 (cloth : alk. paper) | ISBN 9780817391164 (e book)
Subjects: LCSH: Davis, Jefferson, 1808–1889. | Confederate States of America—Politics and government. | Confederate States of America. President. | United States—History—Civil War, 1861–1865.
Classification: LCC E487 .A84 2017 | DDC 973.713092—dc23
LC record available at https://lccn.loc.gov/2016040699

For Ross Smith, Brad Eaton, Sam Lee, and everyone who misses them.

Contents

Acknowledgments

Academia puts a premium on scholarly work that is credited to a single author. In my experience, many support systems have to be present to enable the type of focus, time, and energy necessary to engage in any scholarly endeavor and this book is no exception. This book would not have been possible without the support of my family, colleagues, friends, and a variety of institutions. In this truncated acknowledgment section I will attempt to say thank you to the folks that had a direct impact on my ability to develop this project with the full understanding that there are certainly additional folks that worked behind the scenes that I may not even know about.

My work on Jefferson Davis started in the department of communication studies at the University of Georgia. I distinctly remember the Friday departmental happy hour that led to my initial research into Davis's public discourse. In a conversation over cheap domestic beers at Tasty World, Dr. John Murphy suggested that before I waded into the contemporary debates over the rhetoric of Southern identity that I should consider starting with the public discourse of the Confederacy and that the speeches of Jefferson Davis seemed like an appropriate place to begin that investigation. Despite the fact that nineteenth century public address was a tad outside his wheelhouse, Dr. Murphy was and has continued to be a phenomenal resource. He was not only willing to read draft after draft of my chapters but he was also willing to dive into the public discourse of the period on his own time to help me better understand the context of the rhetorical strategies swirling through Davis's discourse. This project simply could not have happened without his sustained attention.

Beyond the dedicated efforts of Dr. Murphy, many others were crucial in helping me develop a vision for the project. Drs. Celeste Condit, Vanessa Beasley, and Edward Panetta provided key insights into the development of the argument from a descriptive analysis of Davis's rhetorical strategies to a substantive argument about Davis's rhetorical leadership. Dr. John Inscoe is one of the preeminent scholars of the Civil War and generously agreed to advise me on my work on top of his other professional obligations. If this book has any appeal beyond scholars of rhetoric then it is entirely a result of Dr. Inscoe's willingness to help me make connections to the wider audiences interested in studying the Civil War.

I have had the privilege of working with a series of colleagues who have been incredibly supportive of this project. At Trinity University I enjoyed countless conversations with Drs. Kyle Gillette, Andrew Hansen, Brooks Hill, and John McGrath. At Wake Forest University I have relied heavily on my colleagues in the Department of Communication broadly and the rhetoricians in particular to help with the preparation of this book. I could not have accomplished that without key conversations with Drs. John Llewellyn, Ron Von Burg, Alessandra Beasley Von Burg, and Meg Zulick. In particular, I would like to thank Dr. Michael Hyde for serving as my mentor, colleague, and friend. His willingness to help junior faculty develop better arguments and become better writers is inspiring, and all of us who have benefitted from his counsel have an obligation to pay it forward to future generations of young scholars.

As a director of debate I can testify that it is almost impossible to balance the demands of directing a debate program with traditional academic research without a robust coaching staff who are willing to go above and beyond to provide opportunities for the director to step away and write. I cannot overestimate how lucky I have been to work with such a dedicated group of coaches and assistant coaches. When I first arrived at Wake Forest, J. P. Lacy and Alex Lamballe worked countless hours to help me with the transition back to the team while allowing me space to continue to work on this project. After J. P. and Alex, no one shouldered more of the burden of my scholarly work than Len Neighbors and Justin Green. Len joined Wake Debate and single-handedly imposed order on chaos by developing a set of protocols and systems that transitioned my daily life from a series of unpredictable crises to a *more* predictable set of priorities that for the first time included time for scholarship. Justin returned to Wake Debate to show us once again the path to competitive success in the fast-paced changing world of intercollegiate debate. Justin's commitment to our debaters is unmatched and as a result I have had opportunities to focus on my writing while he listened to practice speeches and worked with our debaters to maintain the competitive success that we expect at Wake Forest debate. Throughout my entire time at Wake Forest I have also been incredibly lucky to have a series of graduate assistant coaches that have worked in the trenches day in and day out. We could not operate a squad of our size with our success without their daily sacrifices.

Speaking of daily sacrifices, I have had the benefit of working with the best administrative support a person could ask for: Virginia Bannigan, Candice Burris, Patty Lanier, Jo Lowe, Lupita Puente, and Holly Stearne. They have all provided incredible support to help me as I pursued this project. A former department chair of mine once said that faculty come and go so the real measure of a successful department is the quality of the administrative support. It is the hard work of these folks that have definitely made it possible for me to focus on this project and be a part of successful departments.

Beyond my professional world, I have benefitted from a series of close friendships with brilliant people that have been a constant source of encouragement. Drew Shermeta, Dr. Kristen McCauliff, Cagney Gentry, Alison Shermeta, Dr. Patrick Keating, and Lisa Jasinski have shared countless meals, vacations, and late night conversations that have helped me realize just how important it is to have friends who help share in the triumphs and the defeats. Drs. Calum Matheson and Chris Lundberg have been phenomenal colleagues who have demonstrated to me the power within the debate community for folks to move beyond competitors and to support each other as friends. Even though we have not been in the same city for over a decade, Dr. Ken Rufo has been a close friend and coauthor who has taken the time to contemplate and respond to every argument I have ever uttered. Every academic has to have a friend who they can count on for a brutally honest assessment and Ken is that person for me. Seth Gannon and Nate Cohn were essential compatriots in this project as my writing retreat partners. Their dedication to their crafts is unparalleled and their commitment to our writing retreats kept me accountable at key moments. Seth Gannon, in particular, was a godsend. Seth volunteered to copyedit every draft of this project while providing key suggestions that helped develop my voice as a writer. I simply cannot thank him enough for his help. Dr. Michael Lee and Erin Benson have been a constant source of inspiration, intellectual encouragement, and humor as they serve as a daily reminder of how important it is to keep perspective on the things in life that really matter.

I have had the honor and privilege of working with two of the best mentors possible. Both of them are former directors of debate who have gone on to become leaders in their institutions and in our discipline. Dr. Ed Panetta at the University of Georgia helped guide my transition from an assistant coach focused on individual wins to a director of debate responsible for the long-term vision of the program. He was patient with me as I struggled with that difficult transition that requires letting go of some of the parts of being a debate coach that draw more community praise while developing a program of scholarship that is necessary to protect a debate program in the long run. He has been a coauthor and friend throughout my work on this project with a keen eye for the strength of any given argument.

I can safely say that I would not have been able to complete this project without Dr. Allan Louden, because I would not have been an academic without his presence in my life. He recruited me as a high school debater and helped make it possible for me to attend Wake Forest University, where I discovered my interest in the Civil War during Dr. Paul Escott's phenomenal class on the subject. Dr. Louden then encouraged me to consider graduate school rather than my original plan to jump straight into the ranks of high school debate coaching. He has been my counsel for every significant personal and professional decision I have faced since I arrived on campus at Wake Forest in the fall of 1997. Without Dr. Louden's encouragement and support, I would not have been able to contemplate, much less complete, this work.

Last, but not least, my family has been a crucial support system. This project has occupied too many family conversations to count. My wife, Becca, has been my strongest supporter on this project and every other component of my personal and professional lives. Despite the fact that I travel constantly for debate and she is incredibly busy as the founder and co-owner of a successful business, she sacrificed her time and energy to make it possible for me to disappear to a series of writing retreats. She is the hardest-working person I know and watching her build her business has inspired me to push forward on more than one occasion. Our daughter, Piper, has an incredible role model in her mother. Piper also inspired me to carry on through the waves of edits with her infectious smile and constant barrage of giggles. In addition to Becca and Piper, my brother Justin and my sister-in-law Lisa have stomached countless impromptu conversations about rhetoric, history, and the Civil War. They are both engineers by training so I am sure that they have cringed on more than one occasion, but they have always been incredibly supportive. I am also grateful for the support of my mother-in-law, Rosie, my brothers-in-law Jared and Jonathan, and my sister-in-law Jordy. They have all been a part of the dinners, drinks, and holidays that every academic needs to escape the blinking cursor.

Finally, my parents, Bob and Pam Atchison, have supported every dream I have ever had—including my aspirations to become a professor. My mother's commitment to the Shreveport Regional Arts Council taught me the value of true hard work and the importance of developing creativity as a leadership skill. She is one of the most impressive leaders I know and her hard work will pay dividends for her communities for generations to come. My father is a brilliant business and salesperson who prepared me for the life of rejection that accompanies academia. He taught me that every no is just one step closer to a yes and that persistence often matters more than anything else. He has dropped everything to help me on so many occasions that I cannot keep track of them much less account for them here. I have no doubt that I will never fully understand the depth of their sacrifice over the years.

This book was supported by the John Rogers Faculty Fellowship in the Department of Speech and Drama at Trinity University, a Trinity University Summer Research Stipend, a Graduate School Dean's Award at the University of Georgia, and a Wake Forest University junior faculty sabbatical. I would like to also thank the *Southern Communication Journal* and *Contemporary Argument and Debate*, which published earlier versions of the chapters on Davis's resignation and conditional emancipation.

A WAR
OF WORDS

Introduction

"Has there ever been another historical crisis of the magnitude of 1861–1865 in which so many people were so articulate?"
—Edmund Wilson, *Patriotic Gore: Studies in the Literature of the American Civil War*

By December 20, 1860, Jefferson Davis had built an impressive resume. He had taken advantage of his family's wealth and power to pursue an admirable career at West Point. He propelled himself into the national spotlight as a hero in the Mexican-American War. He used his national fame to forge a political career that included the prestigious positions of secretary of War under President Franklin Pierce and US senator from Mississippi. He was even rumored to be a future presidential candidate for the Democratic Party. These achievements, however, were overshadowed by the events that followed December 20, 1860, when the state of South Carolina adopted an ordinance of secession. On that fateful day South Carolina helped set in motion a political and social rebellion that threatened to dismantle the United States of America. By accepting the Presidency of the Confederate States of America and holding that position throughout the Civil War, sometimes over the objection of his political opponents, Jefferson Davis cemented his legacy as leader of the largest and most destructive rebellion in American history.

The thesis of this book is that as the rhetorical leader of the Confederacy, Davis was shortsighted. Throughout his time as president of the Confederacy, Davis settled for short-term successes at the price of creating more serious rhetorical problems for himself in the long run. This is not to say that he was a poor orator. It is precisely because his skills as an orator were so powerful that there is room to judge how he used them. The record tells of the inspiring speeches in which he persuaded the Confederate Congress and the public at large to agree to controversial wartime policies. As James M. McPherson notes, at several crucial moments in the war when morale reached new lows, Davis was not only attuned to the sentiment but able to step forward and deliver his public back from the brink with rousing speeches.[1] Being a great orator, however, is not synonymous with successful rhetorical leadership.

Rhetorical leadership encapsulates all the responsibilities in articulating a vision for a nation including the core tenets of its identity, the values the nation should hold dear, the principles it should never compromise, and the goals it should seek for its future. Using the language of Benedict Anderson, rhetorical leadership comes forward to announce and sustain an "imagined community."[2] In the context of the Confederacy, those responsibilities fell squarely on Jefferson Davis. No one else held the institutional authority to call the Confederate nation into being, to articulate its core beliefs, and, using those values, to justify the policy decisions necessary for the prosecution of the war. In some ways he benefited from the lack of predecessors. Although he declared the Confederacy to be the true heirs of the American Revolution, he was not constrained by what previous Confederate presidents had said. In other ways he was constrained by the dearth of rhetorical resources available. It is not easy to invent a nation, much less sustain that vision in the face of total war.

That Davis—once known as the Cicero of the Senate—possessed the skills necessary to make a persuasive public argument is undoubted. His struggle, however, was in overlooking the long-term rhetorical work necessary to sustain a sense of Confederate nationalism, in favor of short-term political gains. At the war's key moments, Davis chose rhetorical strategies that were politically expedient, while eroding the foundation of the Confederate identity; by the end the war there was little left to substantiate what the Confederacy stood for. Emory Thomas put this conclusion in grander terms when he wrote, "Had the heavens opened, the waters parted, and the Confederacy achieved independence, the postwar South would have resembled the prewar South in little more than name."[3]

Of course, in many ways, the Union did not look much like the prewar North either. The primary difference is that when the pragmatic demands of war began to change the North, Lincoln had the vision and wherewithal to rearticulate the Union's core values and identity—enabling the nation to grow and change without losing a sense of self. As Garry Wills has noted, we now point to Abraham Lincoln's Gettysburg Address as a defining moment in the formation of our national identity.[4] At Gettysburg, Lincoln understood that it was his responsibility to justify the Union's participation in the Civil War and that "for the sake of the Union" was no longer a sufficient rallying cry. Instead of focusing on short-term policies to strengthen the Union war effort, Lincoln used 272 words to construct an identity that many Americans hold onto today. As Wills describes, we now date the nation to the opening words of the Declaration of Independence (and not the Constitution), precisely because that was what Lincoln needed to shift the nation's foundation and change the meaning of the war. Davis has no speech equivalent to the Gettysburg address. The core tenets of the Confederacy that Davis was so eloquent in describing early in the war, namely states' rights and the institution of slavery, were sacrificed to the war effort, and Davis offered no new foundation. The bold, unilateral rhetorical acts of the Gettysburg Address and the Emancipation Proclamation were met with great resistance throughout the Union. In the end, however, Lincoln worked to change the public discourse in such profound ways that we now cite these rhetorical maneuvers as key moments in American public address. As David Zarefsky has noted, Lincoln "displayed rhetorical genius in working with the materials at his disposal, to frame a vision of equality that could occupy the middle ground between two unacceptable political positions. By achieving both consistency and change in his rhetoric about equality, Lincoln was able also to speak to the ages."[5] Davis did not make a similar investment by attempting to generate a new Confederate identity outside of states' rights and the institution of slavery—even in the most desperate moments when he asked the public to let go of both.

I am not under any illusion that Davis could have delivered any one speech that could have saved the Confederacy from eventual defeat. Just because military defeat may have been inevitable does not dismiss the importance of examining Davis's rhetorical leadership as a vital tool in his efforts to create and sustain a sense of Confederate nationalism. From the beginning of the secession crisis through the end of the war Davis delivered rousing speeches that were reprinted in newspapers throughout the South and circulated in newspapers throughout the North. At pivotal moments Davis used his institutional authority to address a variety of audiences and ask for their support for his bold wartime policies ranging from conscription to conditional emancipation. Although Davis may not have been able to save the Confederacy through the power of his words alone, he did use public discourse to justify and legitimize the wartime policies of his administration in the face of tremendous opposition from both within and outside the Confederacy. This project examines that public discourse to determine the relative success of Davis's rhetorical leadership.

My focus on rhetorical leadership could not exist without the work of scholars who have mapped the general terrain of Davis's leadership skills. There is tremendous scholarship, in quantity and quality, on Davis's military decisions and interpersonal communication with his cabinet, his generals, the Confederate Congress, governors, and the press.[6] In almost every account, the depictions of Davis demonstrate that he was a stubborn and occasionally a petty micromanager; at the same time he was a true believer in the Confederate cause and worked tirelessly through difficult bouts of sickness to do everything in his power to achieve independence. As McPherson notes, "As an administrator, Davis simply could not bring himself to delegate authority."[7] It is possible that Davis's insistence that he examine every receipt, personally answer every memo, and consider every promotion on a case-by-case basis left him without the time or energy to step back and do the rhetorical work necessary to sustain a stronger sense of Confederate nationalism. This book is not the first to argue that having more soldiers on the books, more guns in the warehouses, and more train cars on the rails would not have resolved one of the core problems of the Confederacy—by April 1865, no one knew what they were fighting for.[8]

Paul Escott's *After Secession: Jefferson Davis and the Failure of Confederate Nationalism* offers one of the strongest assessments of Davis's failure to reconcile the role of nationalism for the overall war effort. Escott writes: "Internal dissensions seriously weakened the Confederacy, for there is a clear link between the failure of Jefferson Davis to build a spirit of Confederate nationalism at home and the inability of southern generals to establish Confederate independence on the battlefield."[9] The goal of this project is to build on these well-established investigations into Davis's controversial wartime policies and the damage they did to Confederate nationalism. Escott, for instance, describes how Davis's conscription policy (with its exemptions for overseers and wealthy people who purchased substitutes) generated the "Rich Man's War" label that damaged the sense of honor and patriotism that served as an initial rallying cry for the Confederacy. Examining these wartime controversies is essential for any discussion of Confederate nationalism. Davis was, after all, embroiled in a series of wide-ranging public controversies including his persistent battles with Joseph Johnston, allegations of favoritism including his defense of Braxton Bragg, disputes over the resources provided to the western theater, and his willingness to suspend the writ of habeus corpus to reign in pro-negotiation forces in North Carolina. Indeed, these controversies are critical for understanding the rhetorical obstacles that Davis faced every time he addressed his various audiences including the Confederate Congress and the people of the Confederacy.

Rhetorical leadership, however, is the measure of how well a leader *responds* to controversies with the rhetorical tools available to the position of authority imbued in the power of the presidency—the power of public address. Davis certainly does not deserve sole blame for every controversial wartime decision he oversaw, or every interpersonal battle that found its way to the public, or the basic reality of limited resources (such that any allocation invited critique). The responsibility for rhetorical leadership, however, was not shared: it belonged to Davis and Davis alone.

Over the next five chapters, this book will review key moments when Davis stepped forward with the tools of his rhetorical arsenal to help constitute the Confederate nation. Most of these addresses and messages were considered successes in their moment. Davis was very good at navigating the delicate balance between hope and desperation to garner support for controversial measures. He was able to position the Confederacy as *one sacrifice away* from independence on more than one occasion. With the gift of hindsight we can assess that as Davis "won" these short-term rhetorical battles he also foreclosed critical options he would need later in the war. He would have been better served, however difficult a task, to rearticulate Confederate identity as the nation was, in fact, changing beneath and with him. That type of vision and boldness, exemplified in Abraham Lincoln, is what separates a few brilliant rhetorical leaders from history's many skilled orators.

I

Decorum in Davis's Resignation from the Senate

"They recognized in him (Lincoln) the representative of a party professing principles destructive to 'their peace, their prosperity, and their domestic tranquility.' The long-suppressed fire burst into frequent flame."

—Jefferson Davis, *The Rise and Fall of the Confederate Government*

With the flames of secession fanning throughout the South, Jefferson Davis found himself in a troubling situation. He was a senator from Mississippi who had risen to national prominence to become one of the central spokespersons for the South, but he was also an outspoken critic of the rash and unorganized manner in which secession was unfolding. Despite his initial objections, Mississippi had seceded and left Davis with little opportunity to continue his role in the Senate. Davis was, however, given one last opportunity to capture the attention of his colleagues through his resignation speech.

In twelve paragraphs, Jefferson Davis officially resigned from the Senate in what Hudson Strode considers "one of the most moving and eloquent speeches in American history."[1] Davis was courteous, succinct, and passionate. As James G. Blaine remarked, "no man gave up more than Mr. Davis," because "for several years he had been growing in favor with a powerful element in the Democracy of the free States, and, but for the exasperating quarrel of 1860, he might have been selected as the Presidential candidate of his party."[2] Given the scope of his national prominence and influence, Davis's resignation was a topic of conversation throughout the nation, which made his speech more complicated than a simple goodbye. The speech was delivered with a simple topical construction: an introduction that announced his resignation, a description of his obligation to the state of Mississippi, a concise explanation of the theory and legal arguments for secession, an elucidation of the complete and total sovereignty of Mississippi, and a plea for peaceful relations. The initial simplicity of the speech vanishes with a closer inspection of Davis's rhetorical struggle to thwart the justifications for a military response to secession through an early articulation of his vision for a peaceful separation. That separation, according to Davis, was not only justified, legal, and timely but should be peaceful because of the shared history between North and South and the character of the people of the South.

The End of Equivocation

By 1860, Davis had bolstered his position as a spokesperson for the South by attacking Stephen Douglas's theory of popular sovereignty. He had adopted the uncompromising position that the Supreme Court's decision in *Dred Scott v. Sanford* had secured Southerners' rights to take slaves into the Western territories.[3] Douglas's theory of popular sovereignty allowed for the possibility that the people in the Western territories would vote to ban slavery, a position that was intolerable for Davis and other senators from the cotton South. In the buildup to the election of 1860, these attacks played a crucial role in the sectional divide within the Democratic Party.[4] Davis hoped to present a unified Democratic front in the election of 1860, but the uncompromising nature of the attacks meant that he could not support Douglas as the sole nominee of the party. Davis, therefore, stumped for the Southern nominee for the Democratic Party, John Breckinridge, who was the vice president under James Buchanan. Like Davis, Breckinridge defended a proslavery platform in direct opposition to Douglas.

Throughout the fall of 1860, Davis continued his attacks on Douglas in the name of helping elect Breckinridge to the presidency. Despite his efforts to focus the conversation on Breckinridge, Davis was increasingly confronted with the question of secession. The uncompromising nature of Davis's position on slavery made it difficult for him to dismiss secession as an option of last resort. Rather than answering the question, Davis chose to invest his rhetorical resources in supporting Breckinridge while equivocating on secession.[5]

The election of 1860 forced Davis to reconcile his theoretical position with the realistic prospect of secession. While Douglas's theory of popular sovereignty may have resulted in slavery being outlawed in the territories, Abraham Lincoln's Republican platform supported the complete prohibition of slavery in the Western territories. In the wake of Lincoln's victory, the South looked to Davis for guidance and the North looked to him to assess the likelihood of secession. Both audiences turned to Davis as one of the spokespersons for the South.

Between Lincoln's election in November and Davis's resignation in January, Davis continued to vacillate in his support for secession. In the period immediately following the election, Davis argued for reconciliation and compromise. He told a leading secessionist from South Carolina, Robert Barnwell Rhett Jr., that he doubted that his home state of Mississippi would even consider secession much less follow South Carolina's lead in actually departing from the Union.[6] Davis was surprised when he found out how much support for secession actually existed within Mississippi and how fast secession conventions were being called throughout the South. He was even more surprised at the attitude of his fellow representatives at a special meeting called by the governor of Mississippi, John Pettus, to discuss the prospect of Mississippi's secession. According to William Davis, "For the first time ever, he found himself consistently in the minority and consistently outvoted."[7] Davis opposed the governor's recommendation for an immediate special legislative session. Not only did the governor ignore Davis and call the session but he also asked Davis to act as his envoy and represent his position in support for immediate secession.[8] Davis declined the governor's request, but the message was clear—secession was coming to Mississippi whether Davis supported it or not.

Davis was not present for Mississippi's special legislative session. President James Buchanan had asked Davis to return to Washington to help him construct his last annual message to Congress.[9] Before he left, Davis reiterated his objections but stated that he would follow the decision of the Mississippi legislature.[10] Buchanan's address, meanwhile, failed to satisfy the North or the South. The ensuing Senate debate over its publication generated a more aggressive response from Davis, who found himself increasingly upset at the provocations of his Northern counterparts. William Davis argues that he "abandoned the . . . cautious role he had been playing for the past few months and stepped forward at least into the second rank of the fire-eaters."[11] In the heat of the argument, Davis declared, "Before a declaration of war is made against the State of which I am a citizen, I expect to be out of the Chamber; that when that declaration of war is made, the State of which I am a citizen will be found ready and quite willing to meet it."[12] Additionally, he publicly signed and supported a statement that declared that all hope for the Union was lost and that the Southern states should act in their own interests.[13]

Despite the heated remarks, Davis had not completely converted to supporting secession. Within a week of the debate, there was a proposal to create the Senate Committee of Thirteen, which would be charged with creating a compromise that would avert civil war. During discussion of the proposal, Davis opined that there had been too much anger in the chamber and admitted that he had contributed to the hostile atmosphere.[14] He called on his fellow Senators to rise above the partisan debate. He argued passionately that "men must look more deeply, must rise to a higher altitude; like patriots, they must confront the danger face to face, if they hope to relieve the evils which now disturb the peace of the land, and threaten the destruction of our political existence."[15] Despite his calls for restraint, he was more pessimistic than ever about the possibility of reconciliation. When the Committee of Thirteen was approved, he initially asked to be removed from consideration, but later agreed to serve, stating, "If I could see any means by which I could avert the catastrophe of a struggle between the sections of the Union, my past life, I hope, gives evidence of the readiness with which I would make the effort."[16]

Despite Davis's participation and the public call for compromise, the committee failed to reach any substantive agreement. News that South Carolina had passed an ordinance of secession complicated the committee's task, but South Carolina's actions did not deter the committee from meeting and arguing over a variety of proposals including constitutional amendments and a restoration of the Missouri Compromise. However, after ten days of intense debate, Davis voted for a resolution to adjourn the committee—they had failed to reach compromise.

The failure of the Committee of Thirteen contributed to Davis's growing assessment that compromise was impossible. At the outset of the committee meetings, Davis sponsored a procedural rule stating that the committee would only report items to the full Senate that had both a Democratic and Republican majority in spite of the fact that his Democratic Party held a seven to five majority on the committee.[17] This early olive branch did little to curry favor with the stalwart Republicans. According to William Cooper, despite a variety of proposals from Democrats Crittenden, Davis, Douglas, and Toombs, the Republicans "declined to move at all from their platform declaration against slavery in any territory."[18] Davis would later write, "With the failure of the Senate Committee of Thirteen to come to any agreement, the last reasonable hope of a pacific settlement of difficulties within the Union was extinguished."[19]

By January 4, 1861, Davis's indecisiveness had come to an end. He wrote to Governor Pettus and made him aware of a bill to be introduced in the Senate that would empower the Federal Government to act against any state that seceded.[20] The bill signaled an end to any thoughts Davis had for reconciliation. On January 8, Davis wrote to his friend Edwin De Leon and predicted, "We are advancing rapidly to the end of 'the Union.' The cotton states may now be regarded as having decided for secession. South Carolina is in a quasi war and the probabilities are that events will hasten her and her associates into general conflict with the forces of the federal government."[21] With no hope left, Davis joined a caucus of Southern senators who declared that their states should secede immediately. He would later write, "I was behind the general opinion of the people of the State as to the propriety of prompt secession."[22]

On January 9, 1861, Mississippi became the first state to follow South Carolina's lead in secession. Mississippi adopted its ordinance of secession while Davis was still in Washington, DC. He heard the news but waited in Washington until he received communication from Governor Pettus. Davis had recommended to the Governor that he should remain in the Senate as long as possible to vote against hostile legislation but made clear that he would follow Pettus's orders.[23] The Governor's instructions arrived on January 19: Davis was to return to Mississippi immediately. That left Davis with one final task in Washington—his resignation from the Senate.

Despite the order to leave, Davis could not travel because of his lifelong struggle with trigeminal neuralgia—an extremely painful facial nerve disorder.[24] He had planned to deliver his resignation on January 20, 1861, but was forced to delay a day, because he was too sick to leave his bed.[25] When he did deliver his address, he wore a patch over his left eye because it was so sensitive to light. Despite Davis's delay, his resignation was met with great fervor. Davis's wife, Varina, described the scene in the Senate chamber: "On the morning of the day he was to address his colleagues, the crowd began to move toward the Senate Chamber as early as seven o'clock. By nine there was hardly standing room within the galleries or in the passway behind the forum. . . . Ladies sat on the floor against the wall where they could not find seats."[26]

With the stage set, she wrote that "Mr. Davis, graceful, grave, and deliberate, amid profound silence, arose to address the Senate for the last time as a member of that body. Every eye was turned upon him, fearful of missing one word."[27]

On January 21, 1861, the crowded Senate chamber listened to Davis and four other senators resign their positions. In contrast to Davis's somber farewell, the other resignations included virulent attacks on Northern colleagues and detailed descriptions of the oppression that Southern states had suffered at the hands of Northern senators. For example, according to Alabama's Clement Clay, the Northern antislavery spirit had "murdered southern men . . . invaded the borders of southern States, poisoned their wells, burnt their dwellings, and murdered their people. . . . It exerted all the moral and physical agencies that human ingenuity can devise or diabolical malice can employ to heap odium and infamy upon us."[28] Clay dedicated the majority of his speech to this condemnation based on his perception of a Northern conspiracy to destroy the institution of slavery in the South.

Georgia's Robert Toombs deployed similar venomous language in his final address in the Senate on February 4, 1861. He began his resignation with the pronouncement that "the Union, sir, is dissolved."[29] He then continued, "While the perfidious authors of this mischief are showering down denunciations upon a large portion of the patriotic men of this country, those brave men are coolly and calmly voting what you call revolution—aye, sir, doing better than that: arming to defend it."[30] He declared that "now you see the glittering bayonet, and you hear the tramp of armed men from your capitol to the Rio Grande. It is a sight that gladdens the eyes and cheers the hearts of other millions ready to second them."[31]

Toombs's declaration that the "glittering bayonet . . . gladdens the eyes" stands in stark contrast to Davis's resignation. The crowded Senate chamber had suffered through a string of Southern senators who used the occasion to attack their Northern counterparts and set the stage for war. Perhaps it is not a surprise that Davis would deliver a resignation more sensitive to the legislative body to which he had dedicated so much of his life. After all, the *New York Times* had declared him "the Cicero of the Senate"; as James Jasinski notes, most studies into decorum begin with Cicero's *Orator*, which contains the critical lines, "In an oration, as in life, nothing is harder than to determine what is appropriate. . . . Let us call it decorum or 'propriety.' . . . The universal rule, in oratory as in life, is to consider propriety."[32]

The Rhetorical Power of the Occasion

The stark contrast between Davis's resignation and the speeches of his colleagues invites a deeper investigation into decorum to determine if Davis's address was simply a more moderate version of the same arguments or if his address actually accomplished something more or less for the foundation of Confederate nationalism. Decorum offers concepts that enable critics to grapple with the specific demands of an occasion and in turn the situated nature of rhetoric. As the earlier quote from Cicero demonstrates, decorum's most basic definition is speaking appropriately for a particular occasion.[33] As Michael Leff notes, traditional understandings of decorum trace back to Cicero and focus strictly on the stylistic features of a speech resulting in the subversion of the concept as a purely aesthetic consideration.[34]

More recently, scholars have begun to revive the utility of decorum through deeper investigations into the related concepts of *to prepon* (appropriateness) and *kairos* (opportune moments).[35] By connecting these concepts, scholars have begun to move away from a strictly stylistic and technical understanding of decorum to a broader function that has opened up space for investigations into how rhetors react to particular situations beyond surface examinations into stylistic choices.[36] Leff argues that the nontechnical understanding of decorum "represents the goal of rhetorical culture—the adaptation of all the available resources to encompass concrete situations. Since this goal must change in the face of changing situations, it cannot suffer reduction to formal rules."[37] The contemporary understanding of decorum requires sensitivity to the uniqueness of occasions, a theme that is echoed by many modern scholars of decorum.[38]

The primary benefit to working with the broader understanding of decorum is that it enables critics to consider the interaction between text and its context, rather than simply focusing on style.[39] When examining the external features of a text, the critic can focus on the ways the rhetor responded to the situational factors involved in the speaking event.[40] Although these situational factors are often overlooked in the narrow interpretation of decorum, Robert Hariman observes, "Cicero makes the received system of rules into a means for thinking about how we coordinate words, thoughts, acts, and gestures to behave purposely in shifting social circumstances." He goes on to explain, "The concept exemplifies the rhetorical sensibility that he articulated and defended throughout his treatises on rhetoric: the sensibility of an active mind attuned to its social environment."[41] The connection Hariman draws from Cicero to the social circumstances surrounding a text demonstrates that the narrow definition of decorum does not cohere with the classical definition. Instead, critics should be engaged in studying the rhetorical sensibilities that texts embody. Understanding the relationship between the message and the occasion in which it occurs, therefore, is a prerequisite to making any assessments of the decorous nature of a text. In the case of Jefferson Davis, it is important to begin by considering how his physical presence on the floor of the Senate revealed a rhetorical sensitivity to the demands of the occasion.

Twelve days prior, Mississippi had moved from a state contemplating secession to a state in rebellion. Davis's decision to deliver a speech of resignation was a dangerous one. Davis's wife and Governor Pettus feared that if he did not leave Washington, DC, immediately that he might be arrested, a fear shared by Davis himself. At the time of his address, rumors circulated that the members of Congress who were resigning on behalf of seceded states would be seized before they could escape to their homes.[42] The Senate chamber was also not exempt from physical violence. Congressman James H. Hammond wrote, "I believe every man in both houses is armed with a revolver—some with two—and a bowie knife."[43]

Despite the risks involved, Davis knew that a face-to-face interaction was a crucial component of any civil engagement. Although it would have been possible for Davis to leave and send a written statement for his resignation, his first lines signal an understanding of the formal structure of the occasion: "I rise, Mr. President, for the purpose of announcing to the Senate that I have satisfactory evidence that the State of Mississippi, by a solemn ordinance of her people in convention assembled, has declared her separation from the United States. Under these circumstances, of course, my functions are terminated here. It has seemed to me proper, however, that I should appear in the Senate to announce that fact to my associates, and I will say but very little more."[44] From these opening lines, the audience glimpses Davis's overarching argument, based in propriety, that doing what is appropriate means subverting the urge to follow raw emotion. This is the rhetorical sensitivity that Cicero mentioned—it was propriety that made him willing to sacrifice the short-term benefits of an immediate departure to the overall demands of the occasion.

The physical presence of Davis among his associates was a powerful sign of his trust in the Senate to make rational choices based on deliberation. Davis's willingness to submit himself to the demands of the occasion was a signal to his Northern counterparts that any discussion of military action against Mississippi was beneath the rational deliberation he expected of the Senate chamber. If he had departed for Mississippi without facing the chamber, then he would have been delivering a message that was congruent with the treasonous charges being levied against the seceding states. His physical presence ensured that any action taken against Mississippi and the South would be simultaneously an act against one of their colleagues and associates. Davis announced that his presence in the chamber grew out of a sense of propriety, establishing the importance of the occasion for everyone involved.

The Power of Epideictic Rhetoric

In addition to signaling trust in deliberation, Davis's physical presence in the chamber was a crucial component of his primary rhetorical strategy—defining the occasion as epideictic. Traditionally, epideictic rhetoric refers to speeches that are ceremonial in nature and include dimensions of audience judgment regarding the praise or blame of a subject. As scholars have noted, these simple definitions have produced more debates than the definitions of Aristotle's two other forms of rhetoric: forensic and deliberative.[45] Investigating the varied approaches to epideictic rhetoric, however, has yielded two functions that are helpful in the study of Davis's address—(1) definition/understanding and (2) the shaping/sharing of community.[46]

Davis's opening lines established that the nature of the occasion was ceremonial and not forensic or deliberative. After he formally announced that Mississippi had seceded and established that he thought it was appropriate to face his colleagues, he moved to define the occasion for his audience. He argued, "The occasion does not invite me to go into argument . . . and yet it seems to become me to say something on the part of the State I here represent, on an occasion so solemn as this."[47] According to Davis, the traditional argumentative forms that encourage argument and rejoinder were not appropriate for his solemn occasion. As Celeste Condit argues, "In deliberative and legislative address, interests and individuals in the community openly compete. The inclusion of 'refutation' in these speeches is a content-sign of such competition. In epideictic, such a focus on partial interests is anathema."[48] What is intriguing is how Davis used his speech of resignation, which he establishes as epideictic in the opening lines, as a forum for arguing for the legitimacy of secession including specific rebuttals against arguments for racial equality, unification, and the use of force. The apparent contradiction is resolved by investigating one of the central functions of epideictic rhetoric—definition/understanding.

The power of epideictic rhetoric to explain a social world stems from the functional pair of definition and understanding.[49] The more troubling a situation, the more an audience will seek speech that helps define the event and provide some understanding of the cause.[50] The rash, radical, and rebellious nature of secession had thrust the entire nation into disarray. Davis seized the definitional authority provided to him by the social turmoil in his farewell address to define the events surrounding secession. According to Davis, the epideictic nature of the occasion did not encourage the traditional legislative argument, but the solemn nature of the occasion did justify explanation. Davis's use of epideictic rhetoric, therefore, was very strategic: under the guise of explanation, he could justify secession without having to share the chamber or give his opposition equal opportunity for rejoinder that would have been appropriate in a deliberative argument.

Throughout his address, Davis addressed the arguments against secession and proclaimed his interpretation of compact theory and how it justified secession. For example, Davis argued that Andrew Jackson's response to South Carolina's 1832 Ordinance of Nullification was not analogous to secession, because the "phrase 'to execute the laws' was an expression which General Jackson applied to the case of a State refusing to obey the laws while yet a member of the Union. That is not the case which is now presented." He went on to argue, "The laws are to be executed over the United States. . . . They have no relation to any foreign country. It is a perversion of terms, at least it is a great misapprehension of the case, which cites that expression for application to a State which has withdrawn from the Union."[51] If Davis had attempted to argue the relevance of the 1832 nullification crisis on the Senate floor in the weeks after Lincoln's election, a response from a Northern senator would be appropriate and expected. The appropriate response to a speech of resignation, however, was for his fellow senators to contemplate the rationale for such a solemn occasion. Contemplation is the appropriate end of epideictic rhetoric, not rejoinder.

In addition to definition and understanding, one of the central functions of epideictic rhetoric is the shaping and sharing of community. Although forensic and deliberative rhetoric also have the capacity to shape and share community, Condit points out that epideictic occasions create "opportunities for expressing and reformulating our shared heritage."[52] Farewell addresses by definition require a reformulation of community, because they entail the departure of persons from their positions of power. In the case of secession, the farewell addresses signaled a clear attack on the very definition of the American community as senators left the chamber precisely to become un-American.

Davis's farewell address attempted to establish community built on peaceful relations. Davis made explicit overtures toward a reformulation of his personal relationship with his political enemies. Nowhere is this more evident than in the final moments of his resignation: "I feel no hostility to you, senators from the North. I am sure there is not one of you, whatever sharp discussion there may have been between us, to whom I cannot now say, in the presence of my God, I wish you well." Davis continued, "Whatever offense I have given which has not been redressed, or for which satisfaction has not been demanded, I have, senators, in this hour of our parting, to offer you my apology for any pain which, in heat of discussion, I have inflicted."[53] Davis attempted to leave the Senate without the legacy of animosity that had permeated the congressional debates throughout his tenure and with a new peaceful relationship with his old colleagues.

After offering a change in his personal relationship to his Northern counterparts, Davis sought to establish that the shared history of the United States could provide a framework for a peaceful separation and a changed communal relationship. After recycling old interpretations of the Constitution and compact theory, Davis argued that secession was legal based on critical moments in US history. For example, Davis alluded to another debate over slavery and stated, "I well remember an occasion when Massachusetts was arraigned before the bar of the Senate, and when then the doctrine of coercion was rife and to be applied against her because of the rescue of a fugitive slave in Boston."[54] With this direct reference to the controversy surrounding Anthony Burns, Davis opened old wounds in an attempt to demonstrate how the two nations could coexist. Davis argued: "My opinion then was the same that it is now. . . . I then said, if Massachusetts, following her through a stated line of conduct, chooses to take the last step which separates her from the Union, it is her right to go, and I will neither vote one dollar nor one man to coerce her back; but will say to her, God speed, in memory of the kind associations which once existed between her and the other states."[55] Through this historical analogy Davis signaled his central argument that the community should dictate neutrality over war despite the change in the formal structures of power. For his part, Davis used the example of Massachusetts to demonstrate that he had maintained a consistent position for years. Now that it was his state that had seceded, the North should wish Mississippi Godspeed and allow it to leave peacefully in the same way that he was willing to let Massachusetts go. After using the Massachusetts example as an analogy to justify Mississippi's act of secession, Davis turned to reformulating community in the face of secession.

In the same way that Davis sought a rearticulation of his personal relationship with his colleagues, Davis argued that secession was actually an opportunity to end the hostility between the sections. From Davis's perspective, secession would remove the central tensions between the states, because they would no longer be competing for power in the Federal Government. In order to persuade his Northern counterparts that a peaceful relationship was still important, Davis once again turned to the shared history argument: "I find in myself, perhaps, a type of the general feeling of my constituents towards yours. . . . I therefore feel that I but express their desire when I say I hope, and they hope, for peaceful relations with you, though we must part."[56] This key move allowed Davis to speak beyond the scope of his position to become the embodiment of the people of Mississippi. He concluded this argument by proclaiming that the relations among the people of the two nations "may be mutually beneficial to us in the future, as they have been in the past, if you so will it."[57] Davis's description of a future based on the benefits of the past established the potential for community in the face of secession. Davis did not articulate the specific details of the benefits of the relationship; instead, he allowed the enthymematic argument to access his audience's concerns over trade, raw materials, familial connections, and a wide range of other issues threatened by a complete collapse of the relationship. Through two key functions of epideictic rhetoric, definition/understanding and shaping/sharing, Davis utilized the occasion of his farewell address to model a personal and sectional relationship that encouraged a peaceful separation.

Davis's strategic use of the occasion signals the potential depth of the expanded notions of decorum. Moving from Davis's physical presence to the opportunities provided by the epideictic nature of farewell addresses demonstrates that Davis was acutely aware of the relationship between his speech and the specific circumstances in which he delivered it. As we have seen, this sensitivity was essential to Davis's overall message that encouraged the peaceful separation of the South and a reformulation of the community based on a shared history rather than a shared government. To better understand how Davis framed the occasion we now must turn to his conceptualization of time, another key concept in the study of decorum.

Timing: Kairos and to Prepon

According to Bruce Gronbeck, "Perhaps since the writing of *Ecclesiastes* and certainly since the 5th-century B.C. Greeks speculated about *kairos, to prepon*, and rhetoric, men have believed that 'timing' is part of what makes rhetorical discourse 'appropriate' to an occasion and audience."[58] Studies of decorum have demonstrated that the relationship between timing and propriety cannot be underestimated. In order to make better sense of this relationship, scholars have turned to two Greek concepts: Kairos and to prepon. *Kairos* is often defined as the "opportune moment."[59] Janet Atwill argues that kairos is best understood through a comparison with *chronos,* which concerns the abstract nature of time.[60] Unlike chronos, kairos is concerned with contingency and the ability to seize the perfect moment for an act of persuasion. Atwill notes that for the Greeks, "The opportune moment plays a critical role in the arts of medicine, sea navigation, and rhetoric."[61] For rhetoric, the propriety of a message depends on the speaker's ability to identify the opportune moment and deliver the appropriate message.[62]

Determining the appropriateness of a message involves the Greek concept of to prepon. John Poulakos argues that the sophists offer rhetoricians the concept of to prepon, which he translates as "the appropriate."[63] Poulakos claims that "*to prepon* points out that situations have formal characteristics, and demands that speaking as a response to a situation be suitable to those very characteristics." To prepon is juxtaposed with kairos to demonstrate the importance of examining appropriateness in a given context. He argues, "*To prepon* requires that speech must take into account and be guided by the formal structure of the situation it addresses." Poulakos continues, "Like *Kairos, to prepon* constitutes not only a guide to what must be said but also a standard of the value of speech. In distinction to *kairos*, which focuses on man's sense of time, *to prepon* emphasizes his sense of propriety."[64]

The combination of kairos and to prepon enables a critic to explore a rhetor's sense of timing and, thus, their grasp of one of the critical concepts of decorum. According to Poulakos, "Both the timeliness and appropriateness are rhetorical motifs whose essence cannot be apprehended strictly cognitively and whose application cannot be learnt mechanically. . . . Timeliness and appropriateness are similar qualities in the sense that they render an expression more persuasive."[65] An examination of Davis's use of time reveals that his understanding of kairos and to prepon was tactical in his attempt to establish peaceful relations between the states.

Davis's message moves from the present, to the past, to the future through a structure that reveals his orientation toward the occasion as the opportune rhetorical moment for separation. Davis began his speech by announcing that the state of Mississippi had passed its ordinance of secession and was no longer a member of the Union. Davis positioned secession as a matter of historical fact rather than an ongoing process that he himself was participating in through his speech of resignation. In doing so, Davis oriented his audience toward a particular view of time that supplemented his epideictic frame. Thus, the question was not whether Mississippi should secede—that had already happened. The question became, how should his colleagues regard that act?

The immediate issue that Davis needed to negotiate was the potential use of force to bring Mississippi and the other seceded states back into the Union. Davis was fearful that secession would trigger a war in which the North would have an overwhelming military advantage. Davis did not believe that the North would allow the South to secede peacefully.[66] Writing on January 13, 1861, to the governor of South Carolina, Francis Perkins, Davis stated, "We are probably soon to be involved in the fiercest of human strife, a civil war. The temper of the Black Republicans is not to give us our rights in the Union, or allow us to go peaceable out of it."[67] In another letter to George Jones, dated January 20, Davis wrote, "To us it became a necessity to transfer our domestic institutions from hostile to friendly hands, & we have acted accordingly. There seems to be but little prospect that we will be permitted to do so peacefully."[68] Davis walked into the Senate for the last time with a firm belief that secession could easily trigger a military response. Thus, Davis not only needed to deliver a justification for secession but also needed to denounce the Union argument for using violence against his home state.

Concomitant with his belief that secession would cause war was Davis's fear that the South was not prepared for such a conflict. Having run the War Department under Franklin Pierce, Davis, more than other Southern politicians, had intimate knowledge of how the Union could mobilize to generate war. Davis would later write, "The knowledge acquired by the administration of the War Department for four years, and by the chairmanship of the Military Committee of the Senate at two different periods, still longer in combined duration, had shown me the entire lack of preparation for war in the South."[69] Davis was considered a hard worker and highly efficient as Secretary of War.[70] Under his leadership, the army had increased its numbers from 10,745 to 15,752 soldiers in his first three years.[71] The total number of soldiers seems insignificant when compared to the number of soldiers killed during any one of the major battles during the Civil War; however, the rapid increase demonstrated that the Union had the capacity and organization necessary to create armies.

Perhaps more important than the increased numbers of soldiers, Davis oversaw the transition to new weaponry. Davis introduced a variety of new innovations, including "improved rifle muskets and rifles, the use of Minié balls . . . the substitution of iron for wood in gun carriages, an advanced system of infantry tactics, and the use of heavy guns and large grain powder in the coastal defenses."[72] Davis understood that the Union held a strategic advantage because, according to his assessment, the "foundries and armories were in the Northern States, and there were stored all the new and improved weapons of war. In the arsenals of the Southern States were to be found only arms of old and rejected models. The South had no manufactories of powder, and no navy to protect our harbors, no merchant ships for foreign commerce."[73] Davis's intimate knowledge of the Union arsenals did not put his mind at ease; instead, it made him more sensitive to the need for time.

In order to thwart a military response, Davis needed to present secession as a decorous act worthy of a civilized people that transcended the decades of debate that had led to Mississippi's action. Time was a central component of Davis's rhetorical strategy. Throughout his resignation, time was both used as a strategic weapon to stress the urgency of the moment and as an organizational device that moved his audience through the past while consistently putting his audience into the reality of Mississippi's present condition as a seceded state. Davis began his explanation of the past debates by differentiating secession and nullification. Through the life of John C. Calhoun, Davis argued that nullification was a theory of resistance designed to preserve the Union at all costs. Secession, on the other hand, "belongs to a different class of remedies. It is to be justified upon the basis that the States are sovereign. There was a time when none denied it. I hope the time may come again."[74] By shifting the political theory from the past doctrine of nullification to the current doctrine of secession, Davis began the process of circumventing the Northern arguments for the use of force.

After highlighting the differences between nullification and secession, Davis again turned to the past to address the most famous example of federal government action against a state, Andrew Jackson's threat to use force against South Carolina in 1832.[75] Davis drew a clear connection between past and present, coalescing the two periods into a critical response at the opportune moment. Rather than engage in a lengthy debate over the legality of Jackson's actions, Davis granted that Jackson was justified precisely because at that moment South Carolina remained part of the Union.

A review of Davis's strategy demonstrates that he utilized history to present an argument in defense of Mississippi's present condition, which he performed as the current reality in the opening lines of his speech. In doing so, he changed the calculation for what was argumentatively appropriate, to prepon, in a way that subverted the primary justification for force against his state. As we have already learned, Davis was sensitive to the need for time to develop a stronger Confederacy and build military resources. From a rhetorical perspective, Davis utilized an understanding of time to reorient the discussion away from the potential for secession to a critical understanding of the appropriate response to secession.

The Power of Decorum

From the opening lines of his resignation, Davis declared that decorum demanded that his address be treated as a solemn epideictic occasion. The contrast between Davis's address and the resignations of his colleagues suggests that Davis may have been one of the few Southern politicians that truly understood the military advantages of the North. His experience as Secretary of War helped him understand the difficulties the South would face to win its independence through war. Davis also understood that attempting to justify secession through the deliberative model of the Senate would do little to persuade his Northern counterparts that secession was justified. Within these constraints, Davis addressed the Senate utilizing the rhetorical resources provided to him by the timing and the occasion of his resignation. Focusing on decorum enabled him to cite the occasion as a justification for circumventing the historical debates over the constitutionality of secession while simultaneously thwarting the justifications for using force against seceding states.

Davis modeled a strict conception of decorum because the deliberative Senate model dictated that factions would seek dialogue over conflict and that rationality would prevail over violence. Every scintilla of Davis's appearance and argument were governed by decorum. His resignation sought to preserve the civility of existing institutions while establishing the legitimacy of Mississippi's actions. Decorum, for Davis, was a model of interaction that he desperately needed his Union counterparts to follow if he was going to buy time for the burgeoning Confederacy. Davis's resignation sought to preserve the civility of existing institutions while establishing the legitimacy of the South's actions. Through the address, Davis sought to establish both that secession and his ensuing resignation were the appropriate responses of civilized people.

Through Davis's address we gain a more complex understanding of the functions of decorum in public address. Rather than reducing decorum to a restraining force that limits the rhetor's actions and/or words, Davis's address demonstrates that decorum *can* function to *broaden* a rhetor's options in a tumultuous environment. Although there are certainly some ways in which "appropriateness" can restrict the rhetor's options, decorum is not limited to the speaker in any given situation. Davis's address relied on creating the conditions for his audience to give him the rhetorical space to justify secession. By citing the power of propriety throughout his address, Davis reminded his audience that the solemn epideictic nature of the occasion required them to be restrained in the interaction. That restraint enabled Davis to make a series of arguments that, apart from the occasion, would have triggered a series of aggressive rejoinders by his Republican counterparts. Thus, Davis was able to use decorum to present secession as a matter of fact to be contemplated rather than an unfolding process of political decisions to be debated.

Davis's argumentative development relied on his audience experiencing a profound sadness that would give weight to the solemn nature of the occasion and space for his controversial arguments. Unlike his colleagues in secession, Davis did not rebuke his Northern counterparts. Instead, Davis apologized to them and marked the occasion as so solemn that decorum demanded contemplation rather than argumentation. The recorded reaction demonstrates that Davis was successful in his attempt to constitute the occasion as such a moment in American history. According to the *Daily Exchange*, "He wished to part with his late associates with kindness and good feeling, and if at any time he had wounded the feelings of any one by words spoken in debate, he begged pardon therefor. The retiring Senators then shook hands with many Senators and left the chamber."[76] Varina Davis recorded, "There was scarcely a dry eye in the multitude as he took his seat."[77] According to the *Charleston Mercury*: "Yesterday will be ever memorable in the history of the United States. In the midst of silence that was almost appalling, the Senators of four sovereign States took leave of their fellows. . . . Senator DAVIS's speech was the most affecting of all. . . . There were few dry eyes in the whole chamber above or below, except among the Republicans, and even they shook hands with the seceders."[78] Although the record reflects that Davis was successful in moving his audience to tears, the speech reveals fundamental problems in Davis's vision for the future interactions between the Union and the Confederacy.

Cracks in the Foundations of Confederate Nationalism

Abraham Lincoln concluded his first inaugural address with the poetic lines "The mystic chords of memory, stretching from every battlefield and patriot grave to every living heart and hearthstone all over this broad land, will yet swell with the chorus of the Union, when again touched, as surely they will be, by the better angels of our nature."[79] Although Lincoln would not live to see the reunion, his vision of the nation as a mythical constellation of people connected through a shared history was essential to his prosecution of the Civil War. As Garry Wills has noted, Lincoln crystallized his vision at Gettysburg, but these early lines demonstrate that Lincoln understood the power of shared history in creating a shared community from the outset of his presidency.[80]

Ironically, Davis's resignation from the Senate demonstrates that he also understood the power of shared history. Rather than cite the mystic chords of memory to support cohesion, Davis utilized the shared history in an attempt to justify separation. For Davis, the shared history commanded the two sections to interact peacefully and rationally while seeking dialogue over conflict. Davis's resignation address represents an early explanation of his vision for the Confederate nation: a group of rational people peacefully enacting their rights to separation. The problem, of course, was that the South's overzealous drive to secession would not resemble any of the characteristics that Davis stood for when, on January 21, 1861, he faced the Senate for the last time. In the coming weeks, Davis would assume the official role of president of the Confederacy, and with it, the responsibilities of articulating the content and character of the Confederacy to the world along with building a stronger sense of nationalism for his domestic audience. Davis's resignation reveals the beginning of a tension that would plague his rhetorical leadership from his resignation through the end of the Civil War—how could the Confederacy be a nation built on the principles of deliberation, rationality, and peaceful relations with neighbors when it was created in a chaotic mess of reactionary fear mongering by ideologues who espoused the willingness to go to war as they left public office? Davis's parting words from the Senate previewed this central struggle while also previewing Davis's fundamental rhetorical failure: despite his impressive rhetorical maneuvers, the Confederacy was simply not the nation he proclaimed it to be.

2

Civic Republicanism in Davis's Inaugural Address

"The audience was large and brilliant upon my weary heart was showered smiles, plaudits, and flowers, but beyond them I saw troubles and thorns innumerable."

—Jefferson Davis, *The Papers of Jefferson Davis*

On February 18, 1861, the Confederate States of America inaugurated Jefferson Davis as provisional president. Sworn in on the front portico of the state capitol in Montgomery, Alabama, in front of an estimated ten thousand people, Davis delivered the first official presidential address of the newly constituted Confederate nation.[1] Without a separate Confederate declaration of independence, responsibility for articulating the justification for secession, establishing legitimacy for the new Confederate government, establishing himself in the office, and outlining a vision for how the two nations could coexist fell squarely on Davis's thirteen-paragraph address. In short, Davis was responsible for introducing the content and character of the Confederacy to the world.

Although the task was difficult, Davis did not work in isolation. The whirlwind of secessionist discourse generated complex, contradictory political voices urging the new nation in different directions. The secessionists had won their initial charge, leading the first wave of Southern states out of the Union, but lost ground to moderation as the need to establish a responsible government grew. Moderate voices emphasized the South's philosophical connection to the tenets of civic republicanism, but that conservative tradition was inconsistent with the radical nature of secession. Within this sea of voices, a strong current pushed for unanimity from both sides, but at which extreme? Davis's inaugural address operated within the demands and constraints of this turbulent cultural milieu. William Davis argues: "In many ways, under-less-than-favorable circumstances, it was one of the finest addresses of his life."[2] Although the speech may have been one of Davis's finest, a closer examination reveals that Davis struggled to reconcile the demands of the civic republican tradition with the radical act of secession. Davis's struggle to resolve tensions at this key moment suggested limitations for the civic republican tradition; the seeds of the Confederacy's troubles with nationalism, in other words, may have been sown in the fertile soil of Montgomery, Alabama.

Baptism by Fire-Eaters

After resigning from the Senate, Davis returned to his home state of Mississippi. He arrived in Vicksburg on February 1, 1861, to discover his election as Major General of the Mississippi militia. He accepted the position and contemplated his return to military service as he traveled home to the Brierfield plantation. After the cathartic release that came with leaving Washington, DC, Davis enjoyed his return to plantation life. In a letter to his friend John Callan, Davis wrote, "I feel the strongest desire to pass the remainder of my days in the peaceful useful toil of my little cotton field."[3] But Davis knew that his fate was being decided in Montgomery, Alabama, where delegates from the first seven states of the Confederacy were hard at work laying the foundation for the Confederate government.[4]

Robert Barnwell Rhett Sr., a fierce secessionist from South Carolina, had chosen Montgomery for this convention before Alabama had even seceded. Rhett included the provision that delegates should meet in Montgomery to create the Confederacy as part of South Carolina's Ordinance of Secession. The "South Carolina Program" was designed to have the Confederate government in place before Lincoln's inauguration.[5] Howell Cobb, a prominent politician from Georgia, served as president of the convention that began on February 4, 1861. The convention was charged with writing a constitution, electing a provisional president and vice president, and passing whatever legislation was necessary for the establishment of a working government.[6]

After Davis's Senate resignation, everyone in the South (including Davis) believed he would be appointed Secretary of War for the Confederacy. In addition to having publicly opposed immediate secession, he was a West Point graduate, a celebrated war hero, and had served as the Secretary of War under Franklin Pierce. In fact, Davis reaffirmed his desire to be a military commander in his letter to John Callan, "I think I could perform the functions of genl. if the Executive did not cripple me in my operations by acts of commission or omission."[7]

Yet on February 9, 1861, the delegates voted unanimously to elect Davis the provisional president and Alexander Stephens of Georgia the provisional vice president of the Confederate States of America. The process took less than thirty minutes. According to the *New Orleans Daily Crescent*, "The history of the world affords no instance of the establishment of a new Government so speedily and so successfully as that of the Confederate States of Montgomery."[8] The next day as Davis was clipping roses in his garden, a messenger approached him with an urgent telegram. According to his wife, "when reading the telegram he looked so grieved that I feared some evil had befallen our family. After a few minutes of painful silence he told me, as a man might speak of a sentence of death. As he neither desired nor expected the position, he was more deeply depressed than before."[9]

On February 11, 1861, Jefferson Davis set out for Montgomery as the president-elect of the newly formed Confederate States of America. Over the next four days he would deliver more than twenty-five speeches in cities across the South before finally reaching the Confederate capital. The inefficient railroad path that took him to Atlanta through Tennessee before returning westward to Montgomery gave Davis an opportunity to tour the Southeast while experiencing firsthand the problems with transportation and infrastructure that he would confront as president. He arrived in Montgomery late on the evening of February 16, 1861, and delivered a last impromptu speech from his hotel balcony. Because the next day was a Sunday, he had an opportunity to rest and prepare his inaugural address, which he delivered in the afternoon on Monday, February 18, 1861.

Despite the delegates' best attempt to show a unified front, Davis's election happened as a series of compromises that hardly represented the unanimity the quick vote suggested. While Davis prepared to serve in a military capacity, several of the strongest proponents of secession lined up to fill the top political positions. Edmund Ruffin, Robert Barnwell Rhett, and William Lowndes Yancey had already proven their loyalty to the Confederacy with their fierce defenses of secession. Many believed, however, that Robert Toombs of Georgia was the logical choice for the presidency. He was a revered senator who had made a name for himself defending slavery, attacking Lincoln, and pushing for immediate secession. His name recognition throughout the South made him an easy choice. According to Herman Hattaway and Richard Beringer, "The initial preference of a majority of the Montgomery delegates for Confederate president probably was Robert Toombs."[10] How, then, was Davis elected and Toombs relegated to the position of secretary of state (a position he grudgingly accepted and soon departed)?

The traditional answer is that the delegates, when confronted with the task of constructing a nation that would require legitimacy and potentially international recognition, found moderation. Emory Thomas, for example, argues, "Secession was the nova—that stage in the life of a star when it burns most brightly before rapid extinction—of the Southern fire-eaters. The radicals had no sooner set the revolution in motion than they lost control of it."[11] He continues, "The time for eating fire had passed; moderation prevailed. The Southern leadership at Montgomery sought to present a unified front to still-dubious Southerners, to the Union, and to the world."[12] Thomas's description of the Montgomery delegates finding moderation is supported by the empirical evidence that Davis and Alexander Stephens were elected despite their earlier opposition to immediate secession. Perhaps, however, while material factors supporting Davis's election were at work, ideological ones were as well. A more comprehensive explanation may lie in the connection between the definition of leadership in the Confederate states and the Southern political elite's intense fascination with the American Revolution and civic republicanism.

Civic Republicanism as a (Southern) Performative Tradition

The historians and rhetoricians who have examined the public discourse of Southern political leaders during secession have noted the consistent appeals to the American Revolution. Southern leaders from across the political spectrum pointed to the American Revolution during the debates over states' rights, slavery, and secession. Thomas summarizes the Southern connection to the American Revolution: "Southerners perceived their political circumstances as being parallel to those of the Founding Fathers: both sets of revolutionaries believed that they were dissolving Lockean compacts—the British Empire and the United States of America."[13]

Although the belief that Southerners were the true heirs of the American Revolution is apparent in their political discourse, it is important to consider the political philosophies that the American Revolution produced and their relationship to the foundation of the Confederacy. When examining the American Revolution, scholars have noted that a fundamental shift occurred in the political discourse and philosophy surrounding the nation's founding as multiple idioms became increasingly important for defining the identity of the revolution. Two of the dominant idioms—liberalism and republicanism—competed for ideological control as the new nation struggled to define itself outside of the British monarchy. According to Issac Kramnick, "Liberalism, at its origin, is an ideology of work. It attributes virtue to people who are industrious and diligent and condemns as corrupt privileged aristocrats and leisured gentlefolk."[14] Liberalism was a Locke-inspired vision of society that Jefferson and Calhoun revised and infused in the public justifications for secession. Republicanism, on the other hand, was borne out of dissolving Lockean contracts. The two idioms were often in tension both in the American Revolution and in Confederate secession. Civic republicanism demands the subordination of the individual to the common good, which contrasts sharply with liberalism's celebration of the elevation of the mobile working individual. Both of these forces were at work in the American Revolution and were present in the movement for secession in the South. Both of these forces are present in Davis's inaugural address.

Although Davis worked to maintain some fidelity to both liberalism and civic republicanism, his inaugural address reveals civic republicanism as its dominant rhetorical frame. It is only by examining the fundamental tenets of republicanism that we can see how the delegates at Montgomery, and, in turn, Davis, were empowered and constrained in their efforts to constitute Confederate nationalism based on the experience of the American Revolution.

Historians such as Gordon Wood, Bernard Bailyn, and J. G. A. Pocock have set the groundwork for rhetoricians to examine how concepts such as liberty, equality, and virtue were deployed as topoi in a new American identity based on a unique mix of antiquarian ideals and cautious Whig idealism.[15] The ideological underpinnings of this political philosophy of "republicanism" were not new at all, but the recitation of ancient appeals within modern political structures resulted in a uniquely American vision of government. As Wood notes, "Republicanism meant more for Americans than simply the elimination of a king and the institution of an elective system. It added a moral dimension, a utopian depth, to the political separation from England—a depth that involved the very character of their society."[16] Rhetoricians such as James Jasinski, Stephen Browne, John Murphy, Jennifer Mercieca, Stephen Hartnett, and others have begun the work of tracing out the implications of republicanism for the political discourse surrounding the American Revolution and subsequent moments in American history. Their work has started to develop the notion of civic republicanism as a performative tradition.[17]

Civic republicanism centers on the assumption that people obtain the "greatest moral fulfillment by participating in a self-governing republic."[18] In the ancient ideal, there was little role for government, because every individual would be virtuous, honest, and altruistic. The founders, however, believed that political structures built around the balance between political participation and restraints on decision-making were crucial to the evolution of republicanism.[19] Political structures would be guided by a strict adherence to enacting policies that were beneficial to the common good. Public participation, therefore, was essential, because "in a free government the public good was identical with the people's welfare [and] the best way of realizing it . . . was to allow the people a maximum voice in the government."[20] In Wood's terms, the republican government "by definition . . .

had no other end than the welfare of the people: *res publica*, the public affairs, or the public good."[21]

To ensure that political institutions served the public good, republicanism demanded that elected officials be dispassionate decision-makers who would set aside personal interests for the good of the community. Wood quotes Thomas Paine: "The representatives of the people would not act as spokesmen for private and partial interests, but all would be 'disinterested men, who could have no interest of their own to seek,' and 'would employ their whole time for public good.'"[22] In addition to making dispassionate decisions, leaders modeled virtue and character to help create a virtuous people capable of rational judgment.[23]

The republican vision of government, therefore, relied on a virtuous citizenry capable of making sacrifices in order to preserve the common good. Political leaders would serve the vital role of ensuring that institutions were free of corruption so that the common good would prevail. Thus, self-sacrifice in the name of the common good became the focal point of the new nation's political discourses as it struggled through one of the greatest political experiments in world history. The fundamental tenets of republicanism shaped the foundation of America and generated a rhetorical tradition that has vestiges in today's modern political discourse.[24]

As Murphy explains, one of the reasons for the republican tradition's pervasive influence is its potential to serve as "an interpretive framework, one offered by speakers to audiences in concrete rhetorical situations as members of the community struggle to make sense of events and to render political judgments."[25] It is the interpretive framework offered by republicanism that both empowered and constrained the delegates in Montgomery. Although the traditional narrative that moderate voices prevailed in the Montgomery convention is certainly accurate, reexamining the justifications for Davis's election through the interpretive framework of civic republicanism offers a supplemental perspective based on the South's perceived connection to the American Revolution. The "moderation" discovered at the Montgomery convention is consistent with the fundamental tenets of the political ideology that helped to guide the same American Revolution.

Electing Davis through the Civic Republican Tradition

The Montgomery delegates held the power to choose a leader for their new nation. Unlike most political elections in which parties nominate a few candidates and the total number of available choices is restricted, the delegates had the opportunity to choose from a wide array of candidates that had served in a variety of public offices and military positions, which also harkened back to the American Revolution. According to William Davis, the initial pool of candidates included a large number of names, but the presumption was that a candidate from South Carolina or Georgia would be chosen because of those states' connection to secession and the relative political clout of their officials.[26] The rules of the convention dictated that each of the states would have a vote and the winner would have to carry at least four states.

In an effort to ensure unanimity and present a strong position to the world, the delegates from each of the states canvassed each other to determine if there was a clear candidate. When Toombs heard the initial reports that Davis was leading several states he "staggered from incredulous surprise."[27] He asked for a final confirmation and when he received it Toombs was "mortified but helpless."[28] The Georgia delegates encouraged the other states to support Alexander Stephens for vice president once it became clear that Davis's election to the presidency was inevitable.

Almost every Davis biography and Confederate history characterizes Davis's election as a surprise, because he had been an outspoken critic of immediate secession. There were, however, many reasons to pick Davis. He possessed military and government experience, and he was popular and respected throughout the South including the crucial border states. According to Hattaway and Beringer, "Davis had been on virtually everyone's shortlist, because of his great prominence as a political leader and his image as a moderate who could appeal to the Upper South."[29] After reviewing the role of leaders in the republican vision of government, the choice of Davis over Toombs or any other fire-eating secessionist becomes clearer.

Unlike Davis, the fire-eaters pronounced public hatred of the Union that made these men unfit for leadership, as Wood explains: "A man racked by the selfish passions of greed, envy, and hate lost his conception of order; 'his sense of a connection with the *general* system—his benevolence—his desire and freedom of *doing good*, ceased.'"[30] The ferocious attacks that helped propel the South into secession now marred these candidates, because they suggested the potential for a radical disjunction with the rest of the larger public and thus the common good. In his debate against Alexander Stephens at Georgia's convention on secession in Milledgeville, Toombs demonstrated his hatred for the Union when Stephens suggested waiting for provocation from Lincoln. Toombs encouraged his audience to "strike while it is yet today. Withdraw your sons from the army, from the navy, and every department of the Federal public service. Keep your own taxes in your own coffers—buy arms with them and throw the bloody spear into this den of incendiaries and assassins, and let God defend the right."[31] Instead of an ideologue, civic republicans would look for a candidate who had considered both sides of the issue of secession.

In addition to being dispassionate, Davis followed the republican tradition of publicly renouncing any motivation to become president. As early as January 30, 1861, Davis sent a letter to his friend and Montgomery delegate Alex Clayton asking to be removed from consideration for the office: "I have said enough to justify me in stating that with the limited knowledge I now possess it is not possible to decide as to what it is best to do in relation to the position I should occupy. The post of Presdt. of the provisional government is one of great responsibility and difficulty, I have no confidence in my capacity to meet its requirements. . . . I write as one thinking on paper and say to *you* who will understand me that I would prefer not to have either place, but in this hour of my country's severest trial will accept any place to which my fellow citizens may assign me."[32] Davis's letter to Clayton follows the republican script perfectly: Davis was not confident in his abilities to accept a position with such responsibility and preferred not to have it, but if the office sought him then he would grudgingly sacrifice his cotton fields to serve his nation.

Unlike the fire-eaters who celebrated the opportunity to be part of the Montgomery delegation, Davis stayed at home, content to let the delegation decide his fate. Thus, Davis embodied the classic republican tradition of leaders who do not seek the office but respond to the will of the people when asked to serve the larger public good. Candidates who "sought" the office sought power. They would be unable to put the common good first. In juxtaposition, candidates "called" to the office fulfilled their civic obligations to give up personal interests for the greater good. The notion that leaders would be called to their offices is a defining characteristic of the republican tradition.

Robert Toombs may have been well served to follow Davis's example and stay away from the convention for another reason: the republican tradition emphasized the importance of personal virtue. Wood explains that virtue was the cornerstone of the republican tradition, writing, "Because virtue was truly the lifeblood of the republic, the thoughts and hopes surrounding this concept of public spirit gave the Revolution its socially radical character—an expected alteration in the very behavior of the people."[33] Several accounts, including two from his fellow Georgians Alexander Stephens and Howell Cobb, recorded Toombs's repeated public drunkenness throughout the convention. According to Stephens, Toombs was drunk and boisterous every night by dinner. Stephens described one occasion where Toombs was "tighter than I ever saw him," continuing, "too tight for his character and reputation by far." Stephens went on to say he believed that Toombs's behavior that night removed him from serious consideration with his fellow delegates.[34] The strong republican tradition would require the first president of the Confederacy to be a virtuous person who could meet the leaders of foreign countries as an equal and serve as an example to the people of the Confederacy.

The American Revolution produced a political philosophy that required leaders to be dispassionate judges and virtuous citizens. The Montgomery delegates believed that they followed in the footsteps of the founders and chose Davis over a host of powerful fire-eating secessionists who had been far more instrumental in creating the conditions necessary for their new nation. The basis for the moderation that permeated the Montgomery convention may have stemmed from a rhetorical tradition that had been passed down from the American Revolution. Civic republicanism helped form the core of the antebellum Southern identity, which centered on honor and virtue, traits that Davis wore on his sleeve, but that the fire-eaters had extinguished in themselves. Although the republican tradition may have helped Davis get elected, it created unique constraints for his inaugural address.

Davis's Inaugural Address and Civic Republicanism

The people of the South and the nation at large had experienced inaugural addresses, but the first inaugural address of the first president of the Confederacy carried special importance. Most of the traditional functions of an inaugural address were amplified given the circumstances. As Karlyn Kohrs Campbell and Kathleen Hall Jamieson note, the importance of inaugural addresses rests in their symbolic function. Inaugural addresses "are an essential element in a ritual of transition in which the covenant between the citizenry and their leaders is renewed."[35] Davis's inaugural address represented a rupture in the peaceful transition ritual that marked the American democratic experiment. Instead of giving Lincoln the opportunity to mend the nation, the seven states represented at the Montgomery convention had seceded. Davis embodied the end of the democratic experiment for the United States and the beginning of a new experiment for Confederacy. For the South, Davis's inaugural address was essential in demonstrating that secession could be a peaceful transition away from the Union with a new covenant between the citizenry and their leaders. For the North, Davis's inaugural address was a mockery of the democratic system that had elected Lincoln constitutionally. From either perspective, Davis's inaugural address would be read with close attention.

Despite the unanimous vote for the presidency, Davis's inaugural address was constructed within a set of complex political discourses. The tension that produced Davis as a candidate in Montgomery represented a larger set of contradictory forces throughout the South. On one end, secessionists had already achieved a radical action in convincing seven states to abandon the Union. The fire-eaters had lost their bid to control the Confederate government, but they still represented a powerful constituency. When rumors circulated that Davis supported compromise and a return to the Union, Thomas Cobb of Georgia wrote, "Many are regretting already his election. . . . If he does not come out boldly in his inaugural against this suicidal policy we shall have an explosion here."[36]

On the other end of the ideological struggle, the model of the American Revolution prescribed cautious conservatism when constructing a nation. The moderate delegates had elected a candidate who had the best potential to negotiate these forces. Davis was not a fire-eater, but he would not acquiesce to Union economic or military pressure. Davis's inaugural address, then, would have to assure the radical Southerners that he would not advocate reconciliation and would be willing to go to war to preserve secession while simultaneously operating within the performative tradition of civic republicanism, which demanded dis-passionate judgment with an eye for the common good. The result was an inaugural address that fulfilled the demands of civic republicanism by obscuring the truth of secession and thus sowing the seeds of discontent that would blossom when the pragmatic demands of war pressured Davis to return to radical action to sustain the Confederacy.

Even a cursory glance reveals Davis's debt to the republican tradition. The address is organized around the three tenets of the tradition: humble leadership, virtuous actions, and enlightened people. A closer examination, however, reveals a deep ideological tension between the tenets of civic republicanism and the justifications for secession based on Lockean contracts. As the clouds parted and the sun shone down, Davis rose to address his large audience. The first words out of Davis's mouth demonstrated his fidelity to the republican tradition. "Called to the difficult and responsible station of Chief Executive of the Provisional Government which you have instituted, I approach the discharge of the duties assigned to me with an humble distrust of my abilities," he said, continuing, "but with a sustaining confidence in the wisdom of those who are to guide and to aid me in the administration of public affairs, and an abiding faith in the virtue and patriotism of the people."[37]

These opening lines accomplish three vital tasks in Davis's fulfillment of the republican tradition. First, Davis is "called" to serve. As James Andrews argues, "Washington, Jefferson, Madison, Monroe, John Quincy Adams were all 'called' by their 'country' or the 'voice of their country' or some unnamed higher power—by implication the 'people.'"[38] The problem, as Andrew highlights, is that Davis was not elected by the people of the Confederacy. In the republican tradition, the participation of the people was vital to establishing the common good. As Murphy notes, the early republican debates often centered on issues of representation, "The Federalists, in particular, were consumed with the issue of the appropriate amount of *distance* between a leader and the people. If the distance was too far, tyranny could result. If the distance was too little, faction and confusion would doom the republic."[39]

Radical action gave birth to the representation that established Davis's presidency. The Montgomery convention represented only seven of the eleven states that would eventually make up the Confederacy. Within those seven states, secession conventions, not the people, appointed the delegates to Montgomery. Secession and Davis's election were hurried to ensure a functioning government before Lincoln took office. This radical approach helped to undermine the very tradition that Davis sought to reconstitute. The Constitutional struggle over representation was designed to ensure reasonable deliberation.[40] The unanimous election of Davis in under half an hour may have shown the world Confederate resolve, but it did not reveal Confederate deliberation. Thus, Davis may have been "called" to the position, but his inference that the people of the Confederacy did the "calling" was presumptuous at best.

The second task Davis accomplished in his opening lines was to ground the Confederate government in three "god terms" of the republican tradition: wisdom, virtue, and patriotism. Davis effectively deployed these terms without resolving their slippery meanings. By starting his address with an emphasis on these terms, he set the interpretive framework for judgment of the Confederacy. The move was strategic (and critical to Davis's later narrative of the virtuous and honorable nature of secession). By connecting the principles of the new Confederate government to god terms connected to the political discourses of the American Revolution, Davis began the work of establishing a vision for the Confederacy based on the earliest days of the American Revolution.

Although Davis deployed wisdom, virtue, and patriotism, his ambiguous use of the terms required a particular perspective on the concepts in order to support their connection to the Confederacy. In other words, a Northern senator would surely see great irony in the president of a group of rebellious states founding a nation on the principles of virtue and patriotism. Terms that had described dedication to the Union by its founders were now being used to rip it asunder. Unlike the British Monarchy in the 1770s, the Union embraced the same ideals as its secessionists. It now fell to Davis to demonstrate Union infidelity to those ideals.

The final task Davis accomplished in his opening was to reduce his agency and shift responsibility for the success or failure of the Confederacy to the people. The republican tradition celebrated leaders—white male leaders who proclaimed a distrust of their abilities, because it meant that they would seek counsel and deliberation, two qualities rarely ascribed to Davis as president. The republican tradition balked at leaders who expressed confidence in their own abilities, because it meant that they were not reliant on the people for establishing the common good. In addition to expressing his humble distrust of his abilities, Davis grounded his faith in the virtuous nature of the people. Later Davis would increase his reliance on religious rhetoric, but here, Davis built the Confederate identity on the people.

One benefit of the republican tradition was that by putting such a primacy on the participation of a virtuous citizenry Davis would have cover if/when the Confederacy struggled. Davis's deployment of the republican tradition reminded his audience that the success or failure of the new nation rested on their virtuous actions and not on his. The problem, again, was that the people had not elected Davis. It was difficult for Davis to have faith in the patriotism of the people when they had so little voice in his election. Moreover, the radical nature of secession and the risks involved demanded a leader with some vision for the future and the success of the government, not a leader who needed consultation with the people to determine the appropriate course of action. After establishing his loyalty to the tenets of the republican tradition, Davis turned to the task of justifying secession and found himself mired in tensions stemming from the political ideology that supported secession.

Absent a Confederate declaration of independence, Davis needed to articulate the argument for secession early in his inaugural address. There were individual state ordinances of secession, but there had not been a justification for secession from the newly formed government. The intellectual history surrounding secession, however, rested on Lockean principles of contracts rearticulated through John C. Calhoun's compact theory, which had produced a new god term for the South—states' rights. As the political conflict over slavery escalated, Southern politicians depended on states' rights to provide protection from critiques of slavery. The legal and political argument for states' rights became sophisticated and ingrained. According to Thomas, "It was a political habit of mind so long and so articulately used to defend the Southern way of life that finally it became inseparable from that way of life."[41]

Given the history of the South's intellectual, emotional, and political devotion to states' rights, Davis could not articulate a justification for secession without compact theory. The problem, however, was that—within this intellectual tradition that posited states had voluntarily joined the compact of the United States and had the right to leave whenever they determined that their individual interests were better served outside the Union—there was little room for arguments concerning a national common good. A "national good" was only established if it was beneficial for every participant in the compact. Davis, therefore, attempted to negotiate the justification for secession through Calhoun within the constraints of the civic republican tradition. Davis's second paragraph was dedicated to this difficult task: "Our present condition, achieved in a manner unprecedented in the history of nations, illustrates the American idea that governments rest upon the consent of the governed, and that it is the right of the people to alter or abolish governments whenever they become destructive of the ends for which they were established." He continued, "The declared purposes of the compact of Union from which we have withdrawn were to establish justice, insure domestic tranquility, to provide for the common defence, to promote the general welfare, and to secure the blessings of liberty for ourselves and our posterity," concluding, "and when in the judgment of the sovereign States now compromising this Confederacy it had been perverted from the purposes for which it was ordained . . . an appeal to the ballot box declared that so far as they were concerned the government created by that compact should cease to exist."[42]

With clear references to the Declaration of Independence and the Constitution, Davis argued that secession was honorable, because the Union had become destructive to the common good of the individual states that made up the Confederacy. As the republican tradition suggests, the will of the people established the common good, discernible in the peaceful appeal to the ballot box. Davis's negotiation of these concepts became clear: secession was legitimate because it was the will of the people.

Davis's attempt to secure a justification for secession within the republican tradition generated two fundamental problems for his first official articulation of Confederate nationalism. First, secession had not occurred through the peaceful appeal to the ballot box. Second, the insistence on the complete sovereignty of the individual states legitimated future acts of secession away from the central government of the Confederacy.

Political Participation and Civic Republicanism

As William Davis argues, the withdrawal of the seven states "had been decided by just 854 men in the seven state secession conventions—157 of whom had voted against secession—all of them had been selected by their legislatures. Without the ballot box ever being used by the population at large, the destiny of 9 million had been decided by 697."[43] Individual states making decisions for their citizens did not represent a problem for the Jeffersonian tradition, because states were supposed to be the perfect reflection of the people.[44] Civic republicanism, however, demanded a powerful role for political participation. Despite Davis's best attempt to describe secession in terms of the civic republican demand for fuller political participation there was never a peaceful appeal to the ballot box. Davis's assertion that it was the will of the people to destroy the Union is equally deceptive. Perhaps more deceptive was Davis's later assertion that "if I mistake not the judgment and will of the people, a reunion with the States from which we have separated is neither practicable nor desirable."[45] Davis obscured the reality of secession in order to sustain his connection to the republican tradition, because the political participation of the common person tried to prevent the very type of action that secession represented—a rash emotional policy that served the interest of a small minority by putting the larger national common good in jeopardy.

The tension between Davis's narrative of secession and the reality of the privilege of secession would later generate one of the largest schisms in the Confederacy. As William Davis notes, "However much Davis might hope to make it look like a popular movement, the fact is that this political revolution, like the one in 1776 which he looked on as a model, was a revolution by a middle- and upper-class minority over issues of property that only mattered to the privileged."[46] The result of this schism would not become manifest until later in the war when Davis would deal with the label "rich man's war," but fractures appeared in the opening lines of Davis's inaugural address.

State Sovereignty and the Slippery Slope of Secession

It is no surprise that two weeks after Davis's inaugural, Abraham Lincoln declared in his inaugural address, "If a minority in such case will secede rather than acquiesce, they make a precedent which in turn will divide and ruin them, for a minority of their own will secede from them whenever a majority refuses to be controlled by such minority."[47] Speaking directly about the Confederacy, Lincoln asked, "Why may not any portion of a new confederacy a year or two hence arbitrarily secede again, precisely as portions of the present Union now claim to secede from it? All who cherish disunion sentiments are now being educated to the exact temper of doing this."[48] Lincoln's sentiment that total state sovereignty legitimated further secession struck at the core of Davis's continued allusions to Jefferson's ideological position: power to the states invites national dissention.

Jefferson believed in state sovereignty because he saw the road to tyranny paved by a strong national government. James Read summarizes, "In Jefferson's synthesis energetic national government meant government in the interest of the few, while defense of liberty and popular sovereignty somehow turned naturally into endorsement of an extreme version of state sovereignty." He continues, "For every important political contest is essentially between the principle of power and the principle of liberty; if the national government represents power, then state sovereignty becomes for practical purposes the embodiment of the principle of liberty."[49]

Civic republicanism, on the other hand, requires sacrifice for the larger good. The two positions could only be reconciled by empowering the individual states to continue to make critical decisions regarding troop and resource commitments based on what they believed to be their best interest. Given the relative homogeneity of the Southern slave states, this tension may not have produced much anxiety during a time of peace. During war, however, the pragmatic demands required sacrifice on everyone's part for the preservation of the national government.

Similar to the problem with political participation, this slippery slope came to fruition in the years after the inaugural address. Throughout the Civil War, Davis found himself embroiled in battles with state Governors over the power of the national government. The Confederacy's ever-shrinking supply of resources required Davis to conscript property, slaves, and soldiers under the republican banner of sacrifice for the national good. Davis laid the foundation for the governors' resentment in his inaugural address by justifying secession based on the discourse of extreme state sovereignty that had permeated Southern politics for decades. He coached them to interpret each request for sacrifice as an encroachment on liberty.

After Davis had justified secession through the will of the people, he turned to his vision for the Confederacy. Once again, however, the republican tradition constrained the process of invention. At a time when Davis needed to articulate the future and identity of the Confederacy, the conservative nature of the republican tradition prevented Davis from moving too far beyond the status quo.

The Confederacy as Simple Farmers

Inaugural addresses are symbolic sites of rhetorical construction. There was a strong expectation that Davis would outline the character and content of the Confederacy for multiple audiences including the Union, nations of the world, border states, and people of the Confederacy. Davis would need a variety of inventional resources given the demands of the occasion. Unfortunately for Davis, civic republicanism as a rhetorical tradition creates restraints on the available discourses to describe the people and government in question because it is fundamentally a conservative approach to politics.[50] Murphy explains that the republican tradition is focused on preservation especially when the "cardinal virtues of the republic are threatened. The concern is not to move forward, but rather to conserve what has been given to us in the face of dangerous passions."[51] Davis's explanation of the future of the Confederacy follows Murphy's description perfectly by focusing on preservation over creation of a new identity for the South.

According to Davis, immediate action was necessary insofar as it would help preserve the status quo. Davis argued that he was "looking forward to the speedy establishment of a permanent government to take the place of this, and which by its greater moral and physical power will be better able to combat with the many difficulties which arise from the conflicting interests of separate nations." He continued, "I enter upon the duties of the office which I have been chosen with the hope that the beginning of our career as a Confederacy may not be obstructed by hostile opposition to our enjoyment of the separate existence and independence which we have asserted, and, with the blessing of Providence, intend to maintain."[52]

Davis's vision of the Confederacy, therefore, was preservation of the status quo. The new government would preserve the current government from the inevitable difficulties that would arise from two nations on one continent. The threat to the cardinal virtues would come from the "hostile opposition" that the Union represented. Davis's language choices demonstrate that the newly minted nation *was* his vision of the Confederacy. According to Davis, the Confederacy had already "asserted" its independence and he intended to maintain the current state of affairs. There was no grand vision for the future in Davis's inaugural. Instead, future actions would be necessary only to preserve the act of secession. Despite the fact that the Confederate government had only been in existence for hours, Davis spoke of it as a fact of history. But who were the people of the Confederacy? According to Davis, the answer rested in the connection between the South's agricultural economy and the civic republican tradition.

Without mentioning slavery, Davis articulated a vision of the Confederacy based on the agricultural roots of the Southern economy. According to Kramnick, the "republican tradition had, to be sure, always extolled economy over luxury. From Aristotle and Cicero through Harrington and the eighteenth-century opposition to Walpole, republican rhetoric linked a virtuous republican order to frugal abstention from extravagance and luxury."[53] Davis's description of the Confederacy obscured the apparent contradiction between the decadence of Southern plantations that depended on the institution of slavery, on the one hand, and the rejection of extravagant living on the other. Instead, Davis described the Confederacy as a group of simple farmers content to share their commodities with the world.

The combination of the civic republican argument for preservation and the Southern economy's dependence on free trade provided Davis the opportunity to articulate a vision for the people of the South. In Davis's summary, the Confederacy comprised an "agricultural people, whose chief interest is the export of a commodity required in every manufacturing country, our true policy is peace, and the freest trade which our necessities will permit."[54] In order to preserve the Southern way of life, Davis defended the preservation of free trade as one of the primary functions of the Confederate government. This staunch defense echoed the connection between civic republicanism and free trade. As Drew McCoy observes, "Despite persistent fears about the corrupting influence of foreign trade, commerce had always played an integral role in the republican vision."[55]

The connection between free trade and republicanism provided Davis the opportunity to articulate a policy of preservation while simultaneously constituting the people of the Confederacy as peaceful productive farmers. But what about the other slave states that had not seceded yet? Davis utilized the republican tradition's emphasis on agriculture and free trade to generate a connection with the other slave states that might also secede. He justified their secession based on the concept of homogeneity.

The republican tradition has long heralded the importance of a homogeneous population to avoid factions within government. According to Davis, other states should be motivated to join the Confederacy. The new states, however, would have to unite in the common identity unifying the Confederacy and be willing to subvert their individual interests for the common good. "To increase the power, develop the resources, and promote the happiness of a confederacy," he argued, "it is requisite that there should be so much homogeneity that the welfare of every portion shall be the aim of the whole. Where this does not exist, antagonisms are engendered which must and should result in separation."[56] Davis's call for homogeneity is situated within his construction of the Confederacy as a peaceful farming people. In the end, four more slave states would join the Confederacy, but the pragmatic demands of war would validate Davis's concern over factions as he was constantly criticized for not investing enough resources in the western theater of the Confederacy.

After establishing that the Confederacy was constituted by simplicity and peace, Davis turned to war. He ended any question regarding reconciliation when he declared that the South intended to maintain its independence through military means if necessary. Davis reaffirmed the threat that the Union posed and his willingness to meet it directly: "If, however, passion or the lust of dominion should cloud the judgment or inflame the ambition of those States, we must prepare to meet the emergency and to maintain, by the final arbitrament of the sword, the position which we have assumed among the nations of the earth."[57] Once again, he would defend the status quo. The Confederacy faced the "passion or the lust of dominion" of the Union. If it would turn to virtue, the Confederacy could achieve its dreams of simplicity and peace. Unfortunately, even Davis understood that was unlikely. Although the republican tradition helped to thwart fears of the radical coalition, there was a fundamental problem with Davis's continued deployment of the conservative republican tradition: simple farmers rarely won wars.

As Stephen Browne notes of Thomas Jefferson's inaugural address, the republican tradition emphasizes the virtue of simplicity.[58] Davis's address is similar to Jefferson's in that both espoused a vision of simplicity that could not sustain a nation at war. Peaceful, agricultural nations cannot undertake total war. The War of 1812 demonstrated that Madison could not sustain Jefferson's vision of simplicity, and the Civil War demonstrated that Davis could not sustain a vision of the Confederacy as a peaceful agricultural people. War requires organization, industrialization, and resource depletion. Davis's early constructions of the Confederacy as a peaceful agricultural people maintained fidelity to the civic republican tradition, but historically that tradition was not ideal for sustained war.

Success in the Short Term, Conflict in the Long Term

After his inaugural address, Davis took time to celebrate with a series of grand events befitting a presidential inauguration. According to the *Daily Dispatch*, "The inauguration to-day of Hon. Jeff. Davis, of Miss., President of the Confederate States of North America, was one of the grandest Pageants ever witnessed in the South."[59] The *Daily Exchange* documented the scene as follows: "To-night the city is gorgeously illuminated. The President is holding his first levee in Estelle Hall. Bands of music are playing at various points, whilst fireworks and other demonstrations of rejoicing are general throughout the city."[60]

The immediate reaction to Davis's inaugural address was extremely positive and demonstrates that the audience responded well to Davis's rhetorical strategies to invoke the civic republican tradition. William Davis documents, "Responses to the inaugural proved to be almost universally positive. Even Thomas Cobb, never disposed to like Davis, found that it removed many of his doubts. 'The inaugural pleased everybody,' he wrote that night, 'and the manner in which President to Davis took the oath was impressive.'"[61] Louis Wigfall wrote to Davis from Washington, DC, and said, "Your speech was telegraphed & gives great satisfaction. It has the ring of true metal."[62] Beverly Tucker wrote to Davis from Paris, France, and said: "I cannot control the impulse of congratulating you upon your splendid inaugural! It produced a profound sensation abroad, and has done great good to our cause. . . . I wish I could send you some of the notices of the Press, but I am required by the medium through which this is sent to make my package very minute. The London Herald, said among other complimentary things, that 'it was just such a paper as Washington himself might have penned'! And so it was."[63] Some of the reaction to the speech focused on Davis's tone and style. For instance, the *Edgefield Advertiser* noted, "The inaugural address of President Davis . . . will be regarded an admirable paper by every reader of taste. Simple in words, clear in propositions, and firm in views, it will be pronounced by all the very thing for the occasion and for the day."[64] Others highlighted Davis's invocation of the American Revolution, "Davis' inaugural address was chiefly based upon propositions contained in the declaration of the American Independence."[65]

Of particular note is how some newspapers followed Davis's lead and used the civic republican tradition to celebrate his speech as a sign of his impeccable character. The *New Orleans Daily Crescent* wrote, "We have, too, at the head of this Confederacy, the man above all others who is fitted, by nature and by education, for the discharge of the duties imposed upon him and the responsibilities he will have to meet." It continued, "From the telegraphic synopsis of the inaugural Address of President Davis, we infer that he will more than meet the highest expectations of his friends in the lofty and honorable position to which he has been called."[66] The *Anderson Intelligencer* wrote, "The firm, dignified and statesmanlike Inaugural Address of President Jefferson Davis meets the approval of every man we hear mentioning it. Its tone is calm—no bluster, no undervaluing the crisis, and no pandering to enemies of any sort—in a word, the right sentiments and opinions spoken in the right manner."[67]

Such positive reviews, however, are tempered by distance and time. A closer examination reveals that Davis's inaugural address was rife with the same tensions that produced his candidacy. Davis's election is often referred to as a surprise, because other candidates, like Robert Toombs, had more instrumental roles in the movement toward secession and the creation of the Confederate government. However, civic republicanism helps explain Davis's election, as he had a reputation as a virtuous man who preferred rational deliberation to impulsive action. The South was deeply indebted to the civic republican tradition, and Davis's hesitant support for secession became a benefit to his candidacy. His election would signal that the Confederacy was utilizing the rational and deliberative tenets of the republican tradition to choose an effective leader for the new nation. With all performative traditions, however, rhetors are both empowered and constrained by the inventional resources made available. The civic republican tradition that helped elect Davis now presented a unique set of constraints for his inaugural address. Davis was forced to reconcile the radical act of secession with the conservative tenets of the republican tradition. The result was an inaugural address that laid the groundwork for future conflicts that would negatively impact Confederate nationalism.

The longer-term problem for Davis was that he would need to call on the states and citizens of the Confederacy to sacrifice much in the name of the Confederacy, but his inaugural address reaffirmed their basic right to say no. On the one hand, Davis rehearsed the Lockean doctrines that had supported states' rights for decades. Those principles, echoed through Jefferson and Calhoun, posited the primacy of state sovereignty, because the states were supposed to be the perfect reflection of the people. On the other hand, Davis continued to posit the civic republican doctrine of sacrifice in the name of a common national good, which required individual states to subvert their interests in order for the Confederate government to prosecute the war. The result was a tension that manifested itself several times over the course of the war when the pragmatic demands of prosecuting a large scale military campaign required Davis to eliminate states' rights in the name of the Confederate war effort.

In the coming months, Davis would find himself appealing to Confederate nationalism to justify undermining the states' rights principles outlined in his inaugural address. Thus, as the Confederate government struggled to meet the demands of total war, Davis's rhetorical leadership became an increasingly important component of that effort. Unfortunately for Davis, his inaugural address provided rhetorical ammunition for his opponents to challenge his increasingly authoritarian prosecution of the war.

3

Amplification in Davis's Defense of Conscription

"You have been involved in a war waged for the gratification of the lust of power and of aggrandizement, for your conquest and your subjugation, with a malignant ferocity and with a disregard and a contempt of the usages of civilization, entirely unequalled in history."

—Jefferson Davis, *The Papers of Jefferson Davis*

In Jefferson Davis's inaugural address on February 18, 1861, he called for peaceful relations and free trade between the Confederacy and the Union. Less than two months later, at 4:30 a.m. on April 12, 1861, the prospects for peace vanished when forty-three Confederate guns opened fire on Fort Sumter. Although optimists on both sides argued that the war would be short lived, by Christmas of 1862 the battlefield horrors suggested the war would be a sustained conflict with immense losses and few decisive victories. Often on the defensive and almost always outnumbered, the Confederates fought the first two years of the Civil War against increasingly difficult odds. To counter the growing resource disparity, the Confederate government handed down a series of wartime policies designed to improve the chances for winning independence.

Although the policies had mixed results on the battlefield, the aggressive actions eroded the political doctrines that had provided the public justification for secession—particularly state sovereignty. As the pragmatic demands of war increased and Confederate armies suffered greater losses, Davis found his policies under attack from a wide range of audiences. The military objected to his choice of officers, the public objected to a military strategy that appeared too defensive, and several public officials objected to the increasing centralization of power in the Confederate government. Throughout this public criticism, and with the exception of private correspondence with officials who objected to his plans, Davis remained silent. As the battlefield losses and criticism grew, the unity that had propelled the Confederacy into secession was incrementally replaced with a factionalization that threatened Confederate resolve.

Although Davis did not say much in public, he remained sensitive to his role as commander in chief and the power of the institution of the presidency. At the end of 1862, Davis agreed to tour portions of the western army after John Pettus, governor of Davis's home state of Mississippi, implored him to: "You have visited the army of Virginia. . . . At this critical juncture could you not visit the army of the west? . . . Something must be done to inspire confidence. . . . A week spent in Mississippi would greatly improve our situation."[1] Davis began his trip on December 9, 1862, and visited Tennessee, Alabama, and Mississippi. On December 20, 1862, he received an invitation to speak at the Mississippi State House of Representatives. Davis's feeling was "that he had come to work, not to speak; but that he would do in Mississippi what he would not anywhere else."[2] The result was a ninety-minute speech delivered on December 26, 1862. It was Davis's first major speech since the passage of his defining war policies.[3] According to newspaper accounts, "At noon, the hour appointed for the speech of the President, the Representative Hall was crowded to overflowing—not a space large enough to stand upon was left unfilled. The ladies occupied nearly all the seats, leaving the men all standing. The gallery, too, was literally thronged, and many hundreds, perhaps, had to turn back disappointed, so great was the eagerness of our people to hear the President."[4] With the overflowing crowd anxiously hanging on every word, Davis used the occasion to defend a wide range of controversial decisions, including the defensive nature of the Confederate military strategy and the steady erosion of the states' rights doctrine. Of these difficult topics, perhaps the most contentious was the Conscription Act.

The Conscription Act was the first draft in American history. It passed at Davis's request and signaled a fundamental change in Confederate identity. Davis's earlier articulation of the Confederate nation as a peaceful agricultural people with a healthy respect for state sovereignty required considerable revision given wartime policies that demanded a strong centralization of power in the Confederate government and an expanded vision of militarism. Davis's controversial policies required a rearticulation of Confederate values in the face of the increasing demands of war, and—to accomplish this rearticulation—Davis turned to the rhetorical strategy of amplification to construct the Union as a barbarous enemy intent on destruction in an effort to unify the disparate factions of the Confederacy and justify his policy of conscription.

Conscription and Early Signs of Confederate Desperation

By the end of 1861, the Confederacy had taken Fort Sumter and achieved victory at the first battle of Manassas. As Albert Moore argues, the victories in 1861 "produced a wonderfully thrilling sensation throughout the Confederacy, so that the *esprit de corps* of the masses in the summer of

1861 has rarely, if ever, been excelled."[5] By Christmas of 1862, however, the resource disparities between the Union and the Confederacy were having a more noticeable impact on the battlefield. William Davis notes that 1862 had been a tumultuous year for the Confederate Government because of the "inability to follow up Manassas" with "losses at Forts Henry and Donelson, Shiloh, and New Orleans."[6] In addition to these military defeats, William Davis notes that "the failure of diplomatic efforts to achieve speedy European recognition, the exhaustion of the Confederacy's initial financial base, and worst of all the near loss of Richmond and the death of Sidney Johnston" all challenged Confederate resolve.[7]

Given the tremendous losses, it is difficult to find an optimistic perspective of the Confederacy's experience in 1862, but Emory Thomas offers one view: "Every day the war lasted was one more day of Southern independence, and Southerners believed they could win independence by enduring, by outlasting their enemy's will to conquer them."[8] Thomas's depiction of the Southern will to fight puts the 1862 losses in perspective, but its optimism presumes a fundamental ingredient that the Confederacy was finding increasingly scarce—soldiers. The Confederacy could not outlast the Northern will to fight if it did not have sufficient soldiers to defend its territory.

As the end of the first year of the war approached, Jefferson Davis became more concerned about the need for additional soldiers. Early in the war, the Confederate Army was so overwhelmed with volunteers that the government rejected many.[9] The early victories at Fort Sumter and Manassas led to a widespread belief that the war would be won "by a grand march of the Confederate forces to Washington."[10] The opportunity to participate in a quick war for independence attracted many Southern men who were invested in Southern virtues of honor and patriotism. Moore explains: "While enthusiasm was running high, the recruiting of the army caused the Confederate authorities no deep concern. The training and equipping of men, particularly the latter, constituted the really difficult military problem."[11] What changed so dramatically in one year that forced Davis to initiate the first draft in American history? The answer lies in the military strategies adopted by both sides in the wake of the Napoleonic wars.

Until the Civil War, Americans fought wars with small armies that were supplemented by volunteers recruited by governors.[12] According to Thomas, "The Civil War changed all this. Under the influence of Napoleonic military thinking, American generals accepted the need for mass and employed armies much larger than ever before."[13] This shift in military strategy resulted in bigger battles that required more soldiers and a willingness to sacrifice thousands of lives in a matter of minutes. For example, in the famous Confederate blunder of Pickett's Charge, in just fifty minutes 1,123 Confederate soldiers died and 4,019 were wounded.[14] The successful Confederate military leaders—Robert E. Lee and Stonewall Jackson, among others—demonstrated that an outnumbered force could hold its own, but the Confederate Army still needed vast numbers of soldiers if it was to outlast the Northern will to fight.

In addition to the change in military strategy, the length of the war required more soldiers on both sides. Despite the early optimism, the battles of 1861 did not result in a decisive victory for either side. In fact, Civil War textbooks describe 1861 as "Amateurs Going to War," suggesting the relative inexperience of both sides early in the conflict.[15] As the conflict escalated in 1862, it became clear that there would not be a quick military resolution. As Thomas summarizes, "Short-term volunteers, commanded ultimately by governors of individual states, might prove adequate for adventures in Mexico, but military men on both sides of the Potomac realized that if the war continued long, they must have armies which were more than mere amalgams of state militia units."[16] The demand for more soldiers generated a unique policy problem for the Confederate government, which had made a strategic mistake in its enlistment policy.

Against Davis's wishes, the early Provisional Confederate Congress enacted a policy of twelve-month enlistment for the first volunteers into the Confederate Army.[17] By March 1862, with McClellan's army on the outskirts of Richmond, the Confederate Congress saw that the timing for the expiration of these twelve-month enlistments could not be worse. In addition to the threat from McClellan's forces, the defenses of the upper Mississippi River had disappeared with the fall of Forts Henry and Donelson, and Union forces had captured the defenses of the southern Mississippi River, including New Orleans. Despite the gravity of the situation, fewer volunteers were entering in the Confederate Army (in part because original twelve-month enlistees were hesitant to reenlist).[18] As Moore explains, "Absence from home, the privations of camp life, and the arduous duties; they had become painful realities to many persons. The war had not closed, nor had Washington been reached." He continues: "Contemplating a short war, they had rushed off madly to the battlefront without making provisions for the care of their families. . . . Many of them felt that it was only just that they should retire and let those who had not yet served have their turn."[19]

With one-third of the entire Confederate Army potentially retiring during a military crisis, the Confederate government moved into action trying to persuade enlisted soldiers to stay. The Confederate Congress started with inducement strategies including offering $50 and a sixty-day furlough to soldiers who would reenlist.[20] But the horrors of the battlefield and the dream of going home permanently weighed more heavily on soldiers' minds, and the inducements failed. A barrage of congressional legislation designed to improve retention and recruiting followed. Protecting states' rights, however, often became a secondary consideration. The various pieces of legislation created a patchwork of regulations that made it difficult to determine what the exact policy was at any given time.[21] By March 1862, the situation was so dire that Davis turned to mandatory military service.

On March 28, 1862, Davis issued a message to the Confederate Congress requesting: "The passage of a law declaring that all persons residing within the Confederate States, between the ages of eighteen and thirty-five years, and rightfully subject to military duty, shall be held to be in military service of the Confederate States, and that some plain and simple method be adopted for their prompt enrollment and organization, repealing all the legislation heretofore enacted which would conflict with the system proposed."[22] Congress responded by passing the first Conscription Act on April 16, 1862, less than one month before 148 regiments of twelve-month enlistees would disband. Soldiers already serving were now obligated for a three-year enlistment, calculated from their original enlistment date. The Confederate Congress kept the furlough and bounty incentives and even allowed the soldiers already serving to reorganize and elect their own officers.[23] To encourage people to enlist without the stigma of conscription, the Congress granted a one-month delay before the enforcement of the act. There is little evidence that the Confederate government had a formal review to determine the reaction of the soldiers affected by the Conscription Act. As Thomas points out, there were nearly one million white men in the Confederate population who fit the basic parameters of the Conscription Act. Of those, 750,000 were Confederate soldiers at one time or another. The remaining 250,000 are almost all accounted for through the civilian services exempted by the Conscription Act.[24] In other words, the Confederate government was able to utilize the Conscription Act to ensure that the large majority of its eligible white male population fought during the war or served in the civilian sectors supporting the war effort.

The political reaction to the Conscription Act varied and generated fractures across traditional political lines. Even though almost all Confederate newspapers supported the legislation, some proponents of states' rights, including Governor Joseph Brown of Georgia and Vice President Alexander Stephens, fiercely attacked the policy as an unconstitutional usurpation of power.[25] Other states' rights proponents such as Robert

Barnwell Rhett, William Yancey, and Louis Wigfall supported the act as a legitimate exercise of power vested in the Congress of the Confederacy. Other influential leaders, such as Hershel Johnson of Georgia, thought the military necessity was more important than the constitutional debate.[26] In the end, few denied the dire situation the Confederacy faced if it did not retain the service of soldiers that enlisted under the twelve-month program, and fewer yet had a serious counterproposal for review.

It is not that surprising that the Confederate Congress struggled with the Conscription Act. As William Davis summarizes, "For more than a generation, Southern politicians had grown up in the mold, not of policy makers, but of policy critics." He continues, "Like Davis in the Senate, they proposed little significant legislation themselves. Rather, they followed a course of condemning the congressional acts of others. . . . Southern politicians, in effect, had evolved into professional adversaries."[27] It is perhaps this unproductive adversarial process that encouraged Davis to forego serious consultation in his push for the Conscription Act. As William Cooper notes, "He did not launch a great public campaign pointing out the sharp divergence between the country's need and the citizens' willingness to meet it. In contrast, he acted almost stealthily, albeit resolutely."[28] Without a competing solution to the problem, Davis's opponents were forced to accede to his proposal.

Although the Conscription Act had far reaching implications for life in the Confederacy, two exemptions in particular generated a public controversy that struck at the core of the Confederate nationalism. First, the Conscription Act continued the European tradition of substitution, which allowed wealthy Southerners to hire a person not liable for service to replace them in the draft. Second, the Confederate Congress passed the "Twenty-Slave law," which created an exemption to the Conscription Act for anyone who owned twenty or more slaves. Both policies reinforced the antebellum class hierarchy and precipitated the claim that the war was a "rich man's war, poor man's fight." Even though the substitution policy was later abolished and the historical record shows relatively few people who escaped induction through theTwenty-Slave law, the damage to Confederate nationalism is difficult to exaggerate. The Confederate Government squandered an opportunity to demonstrate that individual sacrifice for the common good extended beyond the words of Davis's inaugural address. Instead, the exemptions reinforced the perception that secession was merely an issue of property rights for a small minority who were not willing to risk their lives for the Confederate cause.

Davis's speech at the Mississippi State House of Representatives provided the Confederate nation—as well as the Union and other countries—

a rare opportunity to hear his interpretation of the dramatic events of 1862 and his defense of the Conscription Act. He had been bold enough to force soldiers to fight but not radical enough to challenge the antebellum class system that forced the poor to bear the burden. The military began the war with symbolic victories that inspired Confederate confidence and resolve but lost the strategic edge in a series of battles that put the Confederacy on the defensive. Davis's administration had been the central subject of the criticism with little public response. After nearly two years as president of the Confederacy, he was returning to his home state of Mississippi to inspire confidence in the Confederate cause. (In addition to his rhetorical work, he was bringing troops from Tennessee, redirected to support the Mississippi military cause.) These military and political challenges provided the context in which, at noon on December 26, 1862, Davis rose to address the Mississippi State House of Representatives.

The world had changed significantly since the last time Davis took to the stage in Jackson. On his last visit, he was en route to Montgomery, Alabama, to accept the provisional president of the new Confederate nation. Now, addressing the same audience in the same place, Davis was a different man—the president of a struggling nation. In less than two years, he had helped organize the basic functions of a national government while conducting a war predominately fought on his own territory. He had made controversial decisions that affected the daily lives of everyone in the Confederacy, including the people of Jackson, Mississippi.

Changed man or not, Davis's introduction reestablished his connection to the state of Mississippi. In order to reconcile his position as president of the Confederacy with that of a native son, he announced, "I now, for the first time in my career, find myself the representative of a wider circle of interest; but a circle in which the interests of Mississippi are still embraced."[29] Davis's strategy of ingratiation paid dividends even beyond Mississippi: it established authenticity for all the audiences who might read his speech. According to Davis, speaking to the people of Mississippi, his people, inspired him to the openness with which he had always spoken to them—in a sense, he announced that he was home. Davis proclaimed, "Speaking to you with that frankness and that confidence with which I have always spoken to you, and which partakes of the nature of thinking aloud, I can say with my heart that whatever I have done, has been done with the sincere purpose of promoting the noble cause in which we are engaged."[30] This line is an important textual clue; with his willingness to break out of traditional constraints on official messages and duties, he established his authenticity. Davis utilized the hand-over-heart imagery to establish that these were his unvarnished thoughts. Davis's introduction, then, helped reestablish a connection to his immediate audience while simultaneously generating authenticity for his secondary audiences.

Throughout the address, Davis defended his controversial decisions through a narrative that is typical of war rhetoric—the enemy is evil and going to war is a virtuous response. In a survey of war rhetoric theorists, John Murphy identifies the common theme: "We go to war because it is a practical act and an honorable choice."[31] Robert Ivie highlights the consistent use of savage imagery as a topos of war rhetoric that establishes the morality of the cause and the evil of the enemy.[32] Davis defends the particulars of his war policies, but in a larger sense, he constructs a narrative of an evil enemy to provide a different basis for the war—it is now a struggle for survival against an absolutely evil foe. In order to examine how Davis utilized the savage enemy narrative to justify his conscription policy, we must turn to a discussion of amplification and its connection to Confederate nationalism.

Justification through Amplification

A cursory comparison of Davis's early speeches to his speech from December 26, 1862, reveals an important shift in tone and argumentative style. In his early addresses, Davis strove to embody the civic republican tradition of dispassionate argument and rationality. In his December 26, 1862, address, however, Davis made a series of pathos appeals based on hyperbolic exaggerations of Union forces. According to William Davis, "Gone was the high-flown rhetoric, with barely more than a slim handful of literary or classical allusions or quotes. Though the speech was delivered to legislators, the president clearly aimed it at the people and the soldiery."[33] In this address, Davis relied on a rhetorical strategy that constructed the Union as a wicked enemy that would stop at nothing to destroy the Confederacy—a strategy best understood through the lens of amplification.

According to Richard Lanham, amplification (Greek, *auxesis*) is a rhetorical concept that explains when and why a speaker uses a "heightened word in place of an ordinary one."[34] Using a heightened word can take on many forms, giving the speaker a wide range of options. In fact, according to Kenneth Burke, "Of all rhetorical devices, the most thoroughgoing is amplification. It seems to cover a wide range of meanings, since one can amplify by extension, by intensification, and by dignification."[35] The flexibility that Burke identifies is supplemented by Giambattista Vico's description of the advantages of using amplification in an argumentative setting: "'Amplification' is a certain type of a more elaborate affirmation which, by means of moving the spirits, wins credibility in what must be said. Thus, amplification differs from argumentation because amplification wins credibility by arousing the spirit in addition."[36] Amplification is thus an important rhetorical concept, because it helps identify how rhetors negotiate the process of invention. As rhetors combine thoughts and language, they generate a discourse with points of emphasis that manifest themselves in the text. In his December 26, 1862, address, Davis deployed amplification to address the central controversy over the Conscription Act. In particular, he used amplification in his descriptions of the Union's character, intentions, and resources.

Davis defended conscription by framing the North's intentions as so evil that the Confederacy needed to take radical actions to effectively prosecute the war. According to Davis, the Union planned on total and complete destruction of the people of the Confederacy. Davis, therefore, had to resort to unanticipated tactics to preserve it. He began by assessing the current state of affairs. "You have been involved in a war waged for the gratification of the lust of power and of aggrandizement, for your conquest and your subjugation, with a malignant ferocity and with a disregard and a contempt of the usages of civilization, entirely unequalled in history." Although Davis conceded that the people of Mississippi have been a part of the war, he clarified that they have had the luxury of not *experiencing* the war, "You in Mississippi, have but little experienced as yet the horrors of the war. You have seen but little of the savage manner in which it is waged by your barbarous enemies." In contrast, Davis declared, "It has been my fortune to witness it in all its terrors." After establishing his ethos on the subject, Davis began his list of Union violations: "Old men have been torn from their homes, carried into captivity, and immured in distant dungeons, and where delicate women have been insulted by a brutal soldiery, and forced even to cook for the dirty Yankee invaders; where property has been wantonly destroyed, the country ravaged, and every outrage committed."[37] The irony here is not lost on modern audiences. For Davis, however—utterly ignoring the clear analogy between these complaints and the vile institution of slavery—these infractions on freedom struck at the core of the antebellum hierarchies that defined the social order he had celebrated as the site of Southern strength. Now, two years into the war, he was again using these hierarchies to rally support from his audience.

In order to justify his descriptions of Union atrocities, Davis took assessment of the very character of the people that constituted the Union. According to Davis: "There is indeed a difference between the two peoples. Let no man hug the delusion that there can be renewed association between them. Our enemies are a traditionless and a homeless race; from the time of Cromwell to the present moment they have been disturbers of the peace of the world. Gathered together by Cromwell from the bogs and fens of North of Ireland and of England, they commenced by disturbing the peace of their own country; they disturbed Holland, to which they fled, and they disturbed England on their return. They persecuted Catholics in England, and they hung Quakers and witches in America."[38] In this passage, Davis deployed the amplification-by-extension form referenced by Burke. According to Davis, there were ethnic lineages that created a literal difference between the people of the North and South. The Northerners were the heirs of Cromwell and thus genetically predetermined to replicate their historical injustices on the people of the South. Davis constituted them as a roaming "homeless" group of conquerors looking for their next victims. Amplification by extension was critical to Davis's overall argument; if he could create a rhetorical connection between Lincoln and Cromwell, then he could constitute the Confederate response in terms of the historical battle between good and evil. The Confederacy, by extension, became the heroic agent in a worldwide struggle for peace.

Throughout his address, Davis juxtaposed the character of the people of the Confederacy with the evil of Northerners who took advantage of Southerners in the original United States. He described the people of the Confederacy in two principal ways. First, Davis defended the Confederacy as an honorable people born of the honorable act of secession. Davis argued, "We have chosen to exercise an indisputable right—the right to separate from those with whom we conceived association to be no longer possible, and to establish a government of our own."[39] Davis's description of secession as an "indisputable right" is another example of amplification since the debate over states' rights had raged from the foundation of the country through Davis's career in the Senate. (Here Davis returned to civil republican tradition, describing the decision to secede as a cohesive decision to exercise a right, rather than a radical action by a small minority.) For Davis, then, the Confederacy was a nation of honorable people who had simply tried to exercise an indisputable right.

Second, Davis described the people of the Confederacy as good faith participants in a corrupt system. According to Davis, "After what has happened during the last two years, my only wonder is that we consented to live for so long a time in association with such miscreants, and have loved so much a government rotten to the core. Were it ever to be proposed again to enter into a Union with such a people, I could no more consent to do it than to trust myself in a den of thieves."[40] For Davis, the central weakness of Southern people was their overwhelming love and dedication to the United States, which had been exploited by the Northerners. The juxtaposition with the scheming Northerners is resolved through Davis's hypothetical rejection of another Union. The Confederacy, therefore, was a nation founded by an honorable people who, finally realizing that they were suffering at the hands of their enemies, had no option but to remove themselves—an action for which they were attacked.

After establishing that the people of the Union were violent by nature, Davis turned to framing the events of 1862 in relationship to the Union's overall intentions. According to Davis, the Union was not fighting to reconstitute the United States. Instead, the Union saw the Civil War as an opportunity to conquer and subjugate the people of the South. An earlier quotation, "You have been involved in a war," highlighted Davis's fixation on describing the Union's intentions in apocalyptic terms. He warned his audience that the Union was set on "your conquest and your subjugation, with a malignant ferocity and with a disregard and a contempt of the usages of civilization."[41] In this passage, Davis deployed the amplification-by-intensification form referenced by Burke. Davis combines a set of synonyms with increasing intensity (a strategy of amplification referred to as *synonymia*), culminating in a declaration that the Union's thirst for power is unparalleled in the history of the world.

The attempted conquest of the South was central to Davis's defense of conscription, because it constituted a worst-case, apocalyptic scenario for his audience. Davis made the choice explicit: "The issue before us is one of no ordinary character. We are not engaged in a conflict for conquest, or for aggrandizement, or for the settlement of a point of international law. The question for you to decide is, 'will you be slaves or will you be independent?'"[42] Davis repeated the question, will you be slaves? again in the address. This type of repetition is an important strategy of amplification (Greek, *exergasia*) and helped Davis frame the sacrifices required by conscription as secondary concerns in the grand scheme of Union intentions. In isolation, conscription may have appeared as a tyrannical policy handed down from an overly centralized government, but when compared to the prospect of the enslavement of an entire nation of people, conscription became a necessary wartime policy to prevent a worst case scenario.

Davis's central articulation of the Confederate goal for prosecuting the war, then, became independence through survival. Survival, however, required soldiers. Davis used the story of a Mississippi soldier as a focal point for the sacrifices necessary for the survival of the Confederate nation. He described a sixteen-year-old boy who was shot twice and kept returning to the front line to fight. The boy was struck a third time "and the life-blood flowed in a crimson stream from his breast. His brother came to him to minister to his wants; but the noble boy said 'brother, you cannot do me any good now; go where you can do the Yankees most harm.' Even then, while lying on the ground, his young life fast ebbing away, he cocked his rifle and aimed it to take one last shot at the enemy. And so he died, a hero and a martyr."[43] The visual depiction of a young boy taking his final shot before death is a process of amplification that Perelman and Olbrechts-Tyteca call "presence." They argue that "presence acts directly on our sensibility. As Piaget shows, it is a psychological datum operative already at the level of perception. . . . The thing that is present to the consciousness assumes thus an importance that the theory and practice of argumentation must take into consideration."[44] Presence puts the death of the boy in his audience's mind to arouse them to action and force them to consider the cause for which he died. The answer was the survival of the Confederacy. The Conscription Act enabled Davis to locate more heroes to help win Confederate independence, which was the central goal of his administration. "The great end and aim of the government is to make our struggle successful."[45] Davis, like the soldier, intended to do everything in his power to turn back the Yankee invasion.

In a rhetorical twist on the Union's substantial resource advantage, Davis's speech combined the character and intentions of the Union to construct the Union as a nation built for war: "They had at their command all the accumulated wealth of seventy years—the military stores which had been laid up during that time." Additionally, according to Davis, "They had grown rich from taxes wrung from you for the establishing and supporting their manufacturing institutions. We have entered upon a conflict with a nation . . . vastly superior to us in numbers."[46] In this short description, Davis attributed the Union successes to their longstanding policy of robbing the South of its material resources to support a strong manufacturing base. The Union military successes supported Davis's amplification of the Union's evil character and intentions, because the victories stemmed from the accumulation of vast military supplies. From Davis's perspective, the military supplies were stored with the intention of using them against the South.

According to Davis, the military stores demonstrated the Union's longstanding goal to subdue the South, but it was the Union's military preparations during the war that demonstrated their true dedication to the total destruction of the Confederacy: "In considering the manner in which the war has been conducted by the enemy, nothing arrests the attention more than the magnitude of the preparations made for our subjugation." In particular, "Immense navies have been constructed, vast armies have been accumulated, for the purpose of crushing out the rebellion."[47] Davis amplified the Union's resources by combining a set of hyperbolic synonyms ("immense" and "vast") with a declaration that the Union sought to crush the rebellion. Davis's depiction of the Union as the ultimate enemy became complete—with tremendous resources at their disposal and a goal of subjugating the entire South—because the Union were the descendants of a violent race of people, the Union was truly a wicked enemy.

Unlike Davis's argument concerning the character and intentions of the Union, his discussion of material resources did not easily fit his reductionist binary between good and evil. The Union had a strategic advantage that the South could only begin to match if the people were willing to make tremendous sacrifices. Davis's amplification concerning the character and intentions of the Union helped justify conscription, but he did not provide a clear policy concerning how the Confederacy could ever make up the resource differential that plagued the nation in 1862. He did argue, "Our troops have become disciplined and instructed. . . . Thus, in all respects, moral as well as physical, we are better prepared than we were a year ago," but discipline and training was not the same thing as weapons and food.[48] Instead, Davis turned to Confederate victories to substantiate his argument that the survival of the nation depended on having soldiers ready for battle.

According to Davis, when the Confederacy fielded decent numbers, the moral character of the South ensured victory. He argued, "We have often whipped them three to one, and in the eventful battle of Antietam, Lee whipped them four to one. But do not understand me as saying that this will always be the case."[49] Davis's use of strategic deception here is telling, because his description of Antietam as a clear Confederate victory is far from the truth but fits well within the functions of war rhetoric and the strategy of amplification.[50] According to Davis's narrative, Lee was victorious at Antietam against long odds, but the people should not assume that the Confederacy can continue being victorious against those odds. The primary reason that Davis cited was the depletion of soldiers: "A brigade which may consist of only twelve hundred men is expected to do the work of four thousand. Humanity demands that these depleted regiments be filled up. A mere skeleton cannot reasonably be expected to perform the labor of a body with all its flesh and muscle on it."[51] The metaphor of a starving body may have struck home to hungry Southerners. Davis's description of the Confederacy was now complete—survival depended on the honorable act of supplying soldiers for war. Conscription, then, was *the* crucial element in Confederate survival.

In three critical areas of the war effort—character, intentions, and resources—Davis used amplification to construct the Union as a threat to all aspects of the virtuous Confederate nation. As a result of this strategy, Davis was able to frame the Conscription Act as an essential element in a larger battle between good and evil that required very little sacrifice when compared to the dangers of Union domination.

Amplification, however, was little help in addressing the controversy surrounding the Twenty-Slave law and the "rich man's war" label. After all, if the Union was such a tremendous threat to the very humanity of every person in the Confederacy, shouldn't every person in the Confederacy be a part of the war effort? Davis addressed the controversy by returning to the civic republican tradition that had played such a crucial role in his early articulations of Confederate nationalism. He reminded his audience, again, that he had been called to the office of the presidency as a servant of the common good. According to Davis, he would have preferred to "lead Mississippians in the field, and to be with them where danger was to be braved and glory won," but he was called to the office of the presidency where he now endeavored to help the entire Confederacy.[52] This reminder that he would have volunteered for military duty was important, because it established that volunteering to fight was a virtuous act worthy of celebration. It also demonstrated that Davis possessed the qualities found in a military commander—bravery, decision, and prudence.

After reminding his audience that he had been called to the position, Davis turned to justifying the exemption by redirecting the conversation to the intentions of the policy rather than its effect. Davis declared, "I can say with my hand upon my heart, that whatever I have done, has been done with the sincere purpose of promoting the noble cause in which we are engaged." All of his actions, controversial or not, followed from his desire to secure the virtuous cause of the Confederacy. If, for some reason, a policy was not as effective as it could have been, critics should focus first and foremost on Davis's intent rather than fixating on the policy. His assessment of the controversy surrounding the Twenty-Slave law, therefore, was that the critics were too focused on the policy rather than the intent. The intent of the exemption, according to Davis, was to constitute a "police force, sufficient to keep our negroes in control." If the exemption resulted in more wealthy people avoiding conscription, that was an unintended consequence, not as important as the original intent. Davis declared the intent virtuous and argued, "Had it been otherwise, it would never have received my signature."[53] For Davis, intent was where virtue lay, and the intent was to preserve peace at home. On this level of analysis, the unintended class consequences were subservient to the virtuous intent of the policy.

Amplification and Confederate Identity

Davis's December 26, 1862, address in Jackson was an important speech delivered at a crucial moment in the Civil War. After weeks of public argument that had challenged Davis's wartime decisions, he chose his home state for his public response to his critics. With an emphasis on the rhetorical strategy of amplification, Davis accomplished three tasks in the address: first, he created a new basis for the war; second, he created a new basis for evaluating his wartime policies; and third, he reconstituted the nation as virtuous warriors.

William Davis argues that "only one thing united Confederates—their regional hostility to the old Union."[54] It appears as though Davis's December 26, 1862, address was designed with this constraint in mind. Davis's address centered on a depiction of the Union as a violent aggressor which descended from violent aggressors abroad. According to Davis, the people of the North had long waited for the opportunity to abandon their constitutional obligations and subjugate the people of the South. The resources that the Union had accumulated at the hands of Southerners were finally being put to their intended use, attacking the South with the intention of complete and total destruction. This narrative that described the Union as a wicked enemy at the gate became the new basis for the Confederate cause. According to Paul Escott, "Davis's contention that the Confederacy was the antithesis of the North also implied that independence and not states' rights was the primary goal of the Confederacy. The hostility of the enemy, Davis argued, proved the indispensable need for independence and provided additional reasons to resist."[55] This new basis (which expounded a vision of the Union engaging in total war two years before Sherman and other Union generals are credited with such a strategy) required sacrifice in the name of survival.

To sustain this new basis for the war for his audience, Davis turned to several components of the rhetorical concept of amplification. Amplification enabled Davis to create a heightened sense of urgency that made the sacrifices required by the Conscription Act a natural progression of warfare, given the depravity of the enemy. Davis framed the Confederate losses of 1862 by arguing that the virtuous nature of Confederate soldiers was enough to win early battles, but a shortage of soldiers removed the Confederate edge. In order to prosecute the new basis of the war, the Confederate government took actions to ensure that the young soldiers dying in battle would not perish with able-bodied soldiers waiting at home. How, though, did Davis suggest the Confederate people evaluate his wartime policies?

The second task that Davis accomplished was the elevation of virtue over expediency when judging war policies. Through a return to civic republicanism, Davis argued that the Confederacy was born of virtuous actions and that virtue should guide the nation during its time of war. The Conscription Act was a virtuous policy, because it distributed the burden while maintaining law and order at home. Virtue, then, became the central framework for evaluating Davis's policies. The return to the civic republican tradition was helpful for Davis's appeal to virtue, but it was inconsistent with his new basis for the Confederate war strategy. His inaugural address used the civic republican tradition to construct the Confederacy as a peaceful agricultural people, but now Davis needed a vision of the people that included a warrior mentality. The result was a new Confederate identity. Instead of peaceful farmers, the people of the Confederacy were now virtuous warriors willing to sacrifice anything to save their newfound independence.

Davis's third task required him to articulate his audience as virtuous warriors and describe their roles within the Confederacy's prosecution of the war. Amplification helped Davis prepare his audience for the sacrifices that a sustained conflict demanded. According to Escott, Davis's decision to focus on the barbarism of the Union was important for preparing his audience for the realities of the Civil War: "The stress on northern barbarity was appropriate to the changed circumstances of the Confederacy and had a direct relevance to southerners' state of mind in the second year of the war." He continues, "Despite their expectations, southerners faced protracted war, and Davis sought a way to gird their morale for the long pull and strengthen their determination to resist."[56] As Escott notes, Davis's strategy prepared his audience for an extended conflict. Davis's address went so far as to declare that war was an inevitable component of the Confederate existence: "Cast your eyes forward to that time at the end of the war, when peace shall nominally be proclaimed—for peace between us and our hated enemy will be liable to be broken at short intervals for many years to come."[57] This was the official transition from the peaceful agricultural people who sought free trade in Davis's inaugural address to the new Confederate identity in his Jackson address—virtuous heroes prepared for a perpetual state of war. In the end, Davis proclaimed that the Conscription Act was a moral policy that should be supported by a virtuous people, because there was a wicked enemy at the gate who threatened the survival of the Confederacy.

Davis's Mississippi address gave the blueprint for rhetorical leadership for the remainder of the war. When confronted with a serious public challenge, Davis would remind his audience that the Union was the ultimate enemy bent on total destruction of the Confederacy. Enemy creation is an essential component of war rhetoric that has the potential to rebuild nationalism in the face of domestic dissent.

The response to Davis's speech was varied in some predictable ways. Pro-Union papers attacked the speech and rejected Davis's explanations of the exemptions as pandering to poor whites when it was politically expedient: "As he considers a white man without slaves, a menial not having true dignity, not an equal, it is palpable he thinks there is a distinction. These sentiments he offered when it was not so much his interest to cater to the tastes of the poor white men of the South as it is at present."[58] The reviews throughout the Confederacy were positive and focused on Davis's call for heroism. As an example, the *Chattanooga Daily Rebel* wrote, "Mr. Davis made an eloquent appeal to Mississippians to prove themselves in this hour of peril worthy of the proud fame won by the State upon the plains of Chalmette—to emulate the glory achieved by her sons upon the fields of Mexico, and in the still more glorious battles of the Confederacy."[59]

What is most interesting is how newspapers on both sides of the conflict commented directly on the change in Davis's tone. The *Richmond Examiner*, for instance, argued that Davis's speech reflected the growing trend of amplification, "The custom of denouncing the Yankees is becoming common. Under the soft influences of a serenade, President Davis likens them to hyenas."[60] Pro-Union papers used Davis's change in tone as evidence that Davis was not the "statesman" and "gentleman" that he had been proclaimed to be at the outset of the war. The *Daily Intelligencer* argued, "The smallness and meanness of Jeff Davis has lately been much bepuffed as 'a gentleman,' were never more vividly presented for public inspection than in his late speeches. His poor-spirited vanity and rank malice, which he is petty enough to imagine great qualities, are an exhibition in all their disgusting littleness."[61]

As was the case with his inaugural address, Davis experienced short-term success as the Conscription Acts survived the public backlash. Amplification, however, has its limits, and over the long-term Davis's repeated refrain that the enemy threatened the survival of the Confederacy became less and less persuasive as the Confederacy sacrificed the core tenets that had served as the justification for secession. In short, Davis needed to articulate a Confederate identity worth protecting in the face of a treacherous enemy. Less than a week later, by issuing the Emancipation Proclamation and signaling a fundamental change in the character of the Union, Abraham Lincoln provided Davis an opportunity to do exactly that.

4

Conspiracy Rhetoric in Davis's Response to the Emancipation Proclamation

"The people of this Confederacy, then, cannot fail to receive this proclamation as the fullest vindication of their own sagacity in foreseeing the uses to which the dominant party in the United States intended from the beginning to apply their power."

—Jefferson Davis, *The Messages and Papers Of Jefferson Davis and The Confederacy, Including Diplomatic Correspondence, 1861–1865*

On January 1, 1863, Abraham Lincoln issued one of the best-known rhetorical artifacts of the Civil War. The Emancipation Proclamation—declaring that "all persons held as slaves within any State or designated part of a State, the people whereof shall then be in rebellion against the United States, shall be then, thenceforward, and forever free"—remains central to his rhetorical legacy.[1] The subject of extensive study, it represents a seminal moment in the evolution of Lincoln's perspective on race and America's progress away from the institution of slavery.[2] From a communication perspective, in its form and function the Emancipation Proclamation exemplifies key concepts of rhetoric—the importance of audience analysis in the process of invention, for one. In these decades of sustained critical attention, however, few communications scholars, so focused on Lincoln's famous directive, have examined Jefferson Davis's response.

Three months earlier, on September 22, 1862, Lincoln had offered the "states in rebellion" a final chance to keep the institution of slavery if they were willing to return to the Union.[3] Otherwise he would proclaim the slaves held in Confederate territory free. The deadline was January 1, 1863. Despite this bold September threat, Davis did not comment on the impending Emancipation Proclamation in his December 1862 Mississippi address; instead Davis responded on January 12, 1863, in his message to the Confederate Congress.

One reason Davis's response has received inadequate attention is that it appears predictable. It is nearly self-evident that from the perspective of the Confederacy, Lincoln's proclamation was an illegitimate directive with little moral and even less legal authority. Davis's response, however, went further than simply denying the Proclamation's authority; he used the opportunity to revive the powerful conspiracy discourse that was essential in the creation of Confederate nationalism. In the short term, the appeal to conspiracy helped rally Confederate nationalism. It celebrated the prophetic vision of the fire-eaters, who called for secession as the only measure to protect the institution of slavery. Over the long term, however, as the realities of war forced Davis to propose his own limited conditional version of emancipation, this earlier conspiracy discourse constrained his rhetorical options. These competing functions of conspiracy discourse, enabling and constraining, help explain the precipitous collapse of Confederate nationalism as Davis attempted an impossible move from describing an abolitionist conspiracy in 1863 to defending a limited and conditional form of emancipation in 1865.

Secession and Conspiracy Discourse

Davis's depiction of a radical abolitionist conspiracy had its origins before the war, in the decision to secede. Much of the Southern political discourse surrounding secession centered on an alleged connection between Lincoln and radical abolitionists. Many argued that Lincoln was secretly a radical abolitionist bent on using his executive authority to eviscerate slavery. This grave threat structured the public debate: should the slave states wait and attempt to use their institutional power to thwart Lincoln's aggressive actions, or should they secede before he gained the power of the executive? That Lincoln stated on numerous occasions he was no abolitionist was not only irrelevant but held up as evidence that he was the worst kind of conspirator—a master of language who could use his executive power to craft abolitionist policies without acknowledging his role. Among Southern slave owners, the assumption that Lincoln was beholden to a radical constituency was widely accepted; the only question was whether slave states could leverage their institutional power to prevent radical abolitionist actions by the federal government. Georgia's debate over secession is one of the clearest examples of this conspiracy discourse and shows how it functioned argumentatively.

In the aftermath of Lincoln's election, Georgia held a series of discussions to debate the need for an official secession convention. One set of public debates on secession took place from November 12–16, 1860, in the state capital of Milledgeville. A review of the speeches highlights the narrow range of options that the Georgia political elite believed were available to them in the wake of Lincoln's election. The issue at hand was not whether Lincoln's election had been constitutional. The central question was whether Georgia should adopt a wait-and-see approach or secede before Lincoln took office. Seven speakers addressed this question, including two key figures on opposite ends of the spectrum—Robert Toombs, the presumptive president of the Confederacy who was passed over in favor of Jefferson Davis, and Alexander Stephens, who served as Davis's vice president.

Toombs spoke on the evening of November 13, 1860, and advocated immediate secession. His argument was straightforward: Lincoln's election represented the culmination of a series of events designed to place the abolitionists in a position of power over the slave states. Lincoln's election therefore signaled widespread endorsement of the strongest abolitionist principles. Toombs argued that Lincoln was "elected by the perpetrators of these wrongs with the purpose and intent to aid and support them in wrongdoing." To substantiate this point Toombs said, "Surely no one will deny that the election of Lincoln is the indorsement [*sic*] of the policy of those who elected him, and an indorsement of his own opinions. The opinions of those who elected him are to be found in their solemn acts under oath—in their State governments, indorsed [*sic*] by their constituents." He continued, "Since the promotion of Mr. Lincoln's party, all of them speak with one voice, and speak trumpet-tongued their fixed purpose to outlaw four thousand millions of our property in the Territories, and to put it under the ban of the empire in the States where it exists." He went the final step to argue that the abolitionists would not be satisfied until slavery was completely banned and equality established for African Americans. He summarized, "They declare their purpose to war against slavery until there shall not be a slave in America, and until the African is elevated to a social and political equality with the white man. Lincoln indorses [*sic*] them and their principles, and in his own speeches declares the conflict irrepressible and enduring, until slavery is everywhere abolished."[4]

Once Toombs had established that Lincoln was beholden to a radical abolitionist cause, he argued that the executive had been the last line of defense against the conspiracy to outlaw all slavery. He continued, "The Executive power, the last bulwark of the Constitution to defend us against these enemies of the Constitution, has been swept away, and we now stand without a shield, with bare bosoms presented to our enemies, and we demand at your hands the sword for our defence [sic], and if you will not give it to us, we will take it—take it by the divine right of self-defence, which governments neither give nor can take away." He argued that Lincoln "comes at their head to shield and protect them in the perpetration of these outrages upon us, and, what is more, he comes at their head to aid them in consummating their avowed purposes by the power of the

Federal Government. Their main purpose, as indicated by all their acts of hostility to slavery, is its final and total abolition."[5]

According to Toombs, immediate secession was the only solution to the abolitionist conspiracy. As recorded, the audience was at its most enthusiastic when Toombs asked if they were content to let Lincoln have the total power of the executive, including control of the Army, Navy, and Treasury. After describing the power and prestige of the executive, he asked, "Will you let him have it?" to which the crowd shouted, "No, never!" prompting Toombs's directive to ". . . strike while it is yet today. Withdraw your sons from the army, from the navy, and every department of the Federal public service. Keep your own taxes in your own coffers—buy arms with them and throw the bloody spear into this den of incendiaries and assassins, and let God defend the right."[6] With his thunderous tone, Toombs wrote himself into the history of secession as one of its most passionate, bombastic advocates.

Alexander Stephens presented the case against secession the next evening. Despite being interrupted by Toombs throughout the night, Stephens delivered a plea for reason in the face of uncertainty. In arguing for moderation, he called for appeals based on logos rather than the pathos of Toombs's address the night before. "My object is not to stir up strife," said Stephens, "but to allay it; not to appeal to your passions, but to your reason."[7]

Stephens proposed that Southern politicians thwart Lincoln's agenda through their existing institutional power rather than seceding before Lincoln had even attacked the institution of slavery. He reiterated the constitutionality of Lincoln's election and correctly surmised that if the South seceded in response, history would judge them as traitors. The record reflects that the audience applauded when he declared, "If all our hopes are to be blasted, if the Republic is to go down, let us be found to the last moment standing on the deck with the Constitution of the United States waving over our heads."[8]

Despite this persuasive call for patriotism, Stephens did not invest much energy in denying the conspiracy theory. Instead, he constructed an argument against secession *assuming* the worst possible scenario that Lincoln was secretly a radical abolitionist intent on using the power of the presidency to achieve total emancipation. In fact, he agreed with Toombs that Lincoln was a threat and summarized, "The consternation that has come upon the people is the result of a sectional election of a President of the United States, one whose opinions and avowed principles are in antagonism to our interests and rights, and we believe, if carried out, would subvert the Constitution under which we now live."[9]

What, then, should the South do if Lincoln was secretly an abolitionist? According to Stephens, the South should adopt a wait-and-see approach until Lincoln overstepped his Constitutional authority, providing the South legitimacy to take radical action. Stephens argued, "Let us not anticipate a threatened evil. If he violates the Constitution, then will come our time to act. Do not let us break it because, forsooth, he may. If he does, that is the time for us to act."[10] Stephens cut to the core of Toombs's case for secession by deploying an "even if" argument: even if Toombs's assessment of Lincoln was correct, rash action should wait. According to the record, the audience met him with applause.

Stephens then turned to his own reasoned assessment of the situation, which did not deny Lincoln's true intentions but did deny his ability to act on them. Stephens declared, "I do not anticipate that Mr. Lincoln will do anything, to jeopardize our safety or security, whatever may be his spirit to do it; for he is bound by the constitutional checks which are thrown around him, which at this time render him powerless to do any great mischief." Taking the opportunity to praise the founders, Stephens continued, "This shows the wisdom of our system. The President of the United States is no Emperor, no Dictator—he is clothed with no absolute power. He can do nothing, unless he is backed by power in Congress."[11]

After establishing that the system of checks and balances could prevent radical presidential action, Stephens turned to a detailed assessment of the slave states' power in Congress. He started with the recent gains that proslavery candidates had made in the House of Representatives and concluded that it "is largely in a majority against him." Beyond the raw voting power of the anti-Lincoln coalition, Stephens pointed to more symbolic victories to demonstrate that abolitionism was not as widespread as Toombs described: "Even in Boston, Mr. Burlingame, one of the noted leaders of the fanatics of that section, has been defeated, and a Conservative man returned in his stead." In painstaking detail Stephens denied Toombs's assessment that Lincoln's election demonstrated an unstoppable coalition of radical abolitionists. He concluded his assessment of the House by restating his thesis: "Is this the time, then, to apprehend that Mr. Lincoln, with this large majority of the House of Representatives against him, can carry out any of this unconstitutional principles in that body?"[12]

It was in the Senate, however, that Stephens saw the most potential for proslavery forces to constrain Lincoln. Again he started by describing the political landscape. "In the Senate, [Mr. Lincoln] will also be powerless. There will be a majority of four against him." According to Stephens, the primary implication was that "Mr. Lincoln cannot appoint an officer without the consent of the Senate—he cannot form a Cabinet without the same consent." According to Stephens, without the ability to fill out his administration, Lincoln would be forced into compromise or failure. Again this assessment favored moderation: "Then how can Mr. Lincoln obtain a Cabinet which would aid him, or allow him to violate the Constitution? Why, then, I say, should we disrupt the ties of this Union, when his hands are tied—when he can do nothing against us?"[13]

Although elucidating the potential for congressional restraint was helpful, the decision by Stephens not to engage the merits of the conspiracy made his call for institutional action much more difficult. He acknowledged at the beginning of his speech that Lincoln would try to subvert the Constitution, which was difficult to reconcile with a solution dependent on the checks and balances provided by that same Constitution. In short, his argument relied on a system of public checks and balances that the conspiracy theorists were arguing had already failed. Without a strong denial of the conspiracy, Stephens was left in a defensive position calling for moderation and restraint in the face of an immoderate, unrestrained threat he himself acknowledged.

Stephens's call for moderation stood in stark contrast to Toombs's belief that only removing Georgia from Lincoln's control could impede the abolitionist conspiracy. Toombs's total rejection of a compromise position is consistent with powerful conspiracy discourse. According to Richard Hofstadter, "the paranoid is a militant leader. He does not see social conflict as something to be mediated and compromised, in the manner of the working politician." He continues: "Since what is at stake is always a conflict between absolute good and absolute evil, the quality needed is not a willingness to compromise but the will to fight things out to a finish. Nothing but complete victory will do."[14] Hofstadter's description of the militant leader fits Toombs perfectly. Stephens's call for moderation would have been a more effective strategy if not for conspiracy discourse from a militant advocate such as Toombs. In the face of conspiracy rhetoric's exaggerated depictions of an enemy who will stop at nothing to achieve its nefarious goals, the rhetorical appeal of compromise is greatly reduced.

In the end, Toombs and his pro-secession allies were more persuasive. Georgia did have a secession convention, and on January 19, 1861, the delegates of that convention voted 208–89 in favor of secession.[15] (As noted in chapter two, there were only 854 voters in the original seven state secession conventions. Although Georgia's 208 votes in favor of secession were a significant portion of the total 697 pro-secession votes, Georgia's 89 votes against secession were the vast majority of the 157 total votes cast against secession as well.) The Georgia secession debates set the stage for Toombs and Stephens to become pivotal players in the creation of the

Confederate government. The delegates at the Montgomery convention denied Toombs the Confederate presidency, however, in part because of these rhetorical differences. His bombastic conspiracy rhetoric was essential to the nationalist sentiment that led Georgia to secede, yet Davis and Stephens won the Confederacy's highest offices: as discussed in chapter two, their moderate rhetoric better suited the civic republican tradition that the convention embraced in the wake of secession.

The secession debates in Georgia and the subsequent convention in Montgomery demonstrate the tension inherent in conspiracy discourse: it is a powerful rhetorical tool in the creation of nationalism, but it reduces a leader's options for subsequent calls for pragmatic moderation. Toombs's popularity in the wake of the rash act of secession could not sustain him as a candidate for high office. Stephens, on the other hand, demonstrated the reasoned approach to crisis that made him a good fit with the civic republican tradition. It is with these enabling and disabling features of conspiracy discourse in mind that we turn to January 12, 1863, as Davis confronted the Emancipation Proclamation.

Davis and the Return to Conspiracy

Lincoln had waited for a military victory at Antietam to make the Emancipation Proclamation more palatable to his varied audiences. For Davis, the reverse was true. The military defeat and recent anxiety over his war policies demanded a rally-around-the-flag moment, and the bold move by Lincoln opened up the rhetorical space for exactly that. Looking to bolster Confederate nationalism, Davis took full advantage of the proclamation by returning to the conspiracy discourses that had echoed throughout the South after the 1860 election. In his January 12 message to the Confederate Congress, Davis dedicated five paragraphs to Lincoln's proclamation, which he claimed to know of only because "the public journals of the North" had received it.[16]

Davis began with his policy response: retaliation against Union officers. He turned over authority to the individual Confederate states such that, when commissioned officers were captured, "they may be dealt with in accordance with the laws of those States providing for the punishment of criminals engaged in exciting servile insurrections."[17] As James M. McPherson notes, in many states this was a death sentence.[18] Davis decided that enlisted soldiers, as "unwilling instruments," would be exempt from these charges. Davis considered this policy a measured and appropriate response; in his assessment Lincoln's proclamation stemmed from "impotent rage" at the overall failure of the Union military campaign.[19] Pro-Union papers did not find Davis's proposal measured. According to the *Cleveland Morning Leader*, "Officers taken by the vicissitudes of war may be thrust into dungeons, hung, quartered, or exposed to all the refinements of cruelty which brutalized legislatures of the Southern States have devised for the punishment of State offenders against their peculiar institution." It continued, "Of all the infamous deeds of the rebels, none is more pregnant with the very essence of fiendish hate than this."[20]

According to Davis, the true victims of Lincoln's rage were the very people the proclamation was intended to help. Rather than deploying the traditional proslavery discourse that centered on "civilizing the barbarians" or "bringing Christianity to the slaves" that had become increasingly popular as slavery transitioned from a "necessary evil" to a positive good in the eyes of the Southern elite, Davis declared that Lincoln's proclamation ensured death for the millions of slaves still in the Confederacy. In a less measured tone, Davis argued that "several millions of human beings of an inferior race, peaceful and contented laborers in their sphere, are doomed to extermination." Although Davis did not elaborate on the source of the extermination, he did address Lincoln's request that in exercising their freedom slaves should use violence only as a matter of self-defense. Davis did not mince words. That "insidious recommendation," he said, "encouraged [slaves] to a general assassination of their masters."[21] Davis had revived one of Southern slave owners' greatest fears about Lincoln—that he might, in fact, bring their demise at the hands of their own slaves.

With his "measured" policy response in place and his less measured, somewhat enigmatic threat of total extermination of the entire Southern slave population, Davis focused on rallying Confederate nationalism through a return to secession conspiracy discourse. He accomplished this with a two-part rhetorical strategy. First, he argued that the Emancipation Proclamation was the final piece of evidence demonstrating that the pro-secession forces were correct in their assessment of Lincoln's true character as a radical abolitionist. Second, he argued that the Emancipation Proclamation validated their conclusion that the only way to preserve the institution of slavery was to leave the Union. The Emancipation Proclamation therefore became the final proof of the prophetic wisdom of secession.

After arguing that the Emancipation Proclamation would be a policy failure that would hurt the slaves more than it would help them, Davis introduced a wave of conspiracy discourse by focusing on the symbolic impact of Lincoln's decision. Davis argued, "In its political aspect this measure possesses great significance, and to it in this light I invite your attention." He continued: "It affords to our whole people the complete and crowning proof of the true nature of the designs of the party which elevated to power the present occupant of the Presidential chair at Washington and which sought to conceal its purpose by every variety of artful device and by the perfidious use of the most solemn and repeated pledges on every possible occasion."[22] Thus, Davis began his argument that the Emancipation Proclamation was the final proof that Lincoln had been a radical abolitionist all along.

Davis argued that since the Proclamation could be read by everyone in the North and South that anyone who was hesitant to believe the original conspiracy theory would surely come to their senses as the "whole people" of the Confederacy were now able to see for themselves the "true nature" of the Republican Party. Davis's obsession with using the Emancipation Proclamation as evidence of a larger conspiracy is consistent with Hofstadter's assessment of conspiracy discourse. According to Hofstadter, "The very fantastic character of its conclusions leads to heroic strivings for 'evidence' to prove that the unbelievable is the only thing that can be believed."[23] Davis presents the Emancipation Proclamation as undeniable evidence so self-evident that it need no further discussion, but rather than leaving the audience to derive the implications of this evidence, Davis proceeded to vilify Lincoln as the cunning conspirator that pro-secession advocates identified and attacked during the election of 1860.

Although the vast majority of pro-secession discourse focused on constructing Lincoln as the ultimate enemy of Southern slave owners through a series of racist labels, Davis had been elected, in part, based on a commitment to decorum that established his potential as a statesman for the Confederacy. By this point in the war, his capacity to act as a statesman when discussing the Union had all but vanished. Less than three weeks earlier, Davis had used amplification in his Mississippi address to construct the Union forces as the ultimate evil that would require severe sacrifices to defeat. In response to the Emancipation Proclamation, however, Davis moved from attacking the character of the Union as a whole to attacking Lincoln directly.

Davis's primary attack used Lincoln's own words against him. Davis introduced the conspiracy argument by claiming that Lincoln and the abolitionists had concealed their true purpose through public commitments to preserve the institution of slavery where it existed. Although Davis had a variety of statements from Lincoln to choose from, he chose Lincoln's first inaugural address. According to Davis, inaugural addresses are "the most solemn" pledges taken "under the solemnity of his oath as Chief Magistrate of the United States." In the longest extended quotation of this address, Davis recited two full paragraphs of Lincoln's first inaugural address wherein he addressed the claim that he was an abolitionist. The section includes significant lines such as, "I have no purpose, directly or indirectly, to interfere with the institution of slavery in the States where it exists. I believe I have no lawful right to do so; and I have no inclination to do so."[24] For Davis, these lines served as proof that Lincoln had intentionally deceived the American people into thinking his primary goal was to prevent the expansion of slavery into the Western territories rather than admitting his true goal of radical abolition. According to the conspiracy theory, Lincoln was planning to use the power of the executive to abolish slavery throughout the South. For Davis, the Emancipation Proclamation was not only the final proof of Lincoln's commitment to abolitionism but also his willingness to lie directly to the American people in one of a President's most solemn speeches—an inaugural address. For Southerners, the attack on Lincoln's honor was just as important as the claim that Lincoln's policies were a threat to the Southern way of life. Davis used the South's deep commitment to honor to juxtapose himself to Lincoln. Regardless of any discontent that existed over Davis's prosecution of the war, he could defend himself and his actions as honorable. Davis was, after all, accused of many things, but rarely did anyone challenge his commitment to the cause of Confederate independence.

In addition to the attack on Lincoln's character for his domestic audience, Davis connected with his international audience as well. According to Davis, Lincoln's first inaugural address was not the only moment in which he had expressed his reservations about abolitionism. Davis highlighted official communication between Lincoln's State Department and Great Britain and France wherein Lincoln had allegedly stated that "he was utterly without constitutional power to do the act which he has just committed."[25] Davis was aware that the Emancipation Proclamation would be important to the European nations that had resisted official recognition of the Confederacy. By quoting an official communication between Lincoln and two key potential allies, Davis attacked the credibility of Lincoln's word with these broader international audiences as well.

After citing the Emancipation Proclamation as the crowning proof of Lincoln's involvement in an abolitionist conspiracy and vilifying Lincoln's character for his domestic and international audiences, Davis turned to celebrating the prophetic wisdom of the people of the Confederacy. Davis declared, "The people of this Confederacy, then, cannot fail to receive this proclamation as the fullest vindication of their own sagacity in foreseeing the uses to which the dominant party in the United States intended from the beginning to apply their power."[26] According to the conspiracy theory, the Emancipation Proclamation was an inevitable instrument of oppression that the radical abolitionists had planned from the beginning. That Lincoln did not ask Congress to pass a law and instead chose to issue the Proclamation through the powers of the commander in chief revived the claims of Toombs and others that Lincoln intended to circumvent the hostile Congress that Stephens had proclaimed would protect the interest of the slave states. Lincoln's boldness, therefore, fit the most extreme versions of the conspiracy theories that Toombs and others had warned about in the debates over secession.

Assessing Lincoln's true motive was an important step, but Davis went further to argue that the Emancipation Proclamation demonstrated that secession had been the appropriate action to protect the slave states from the radical abolitionists' inevitable attack. As the Confederate nation struggled with a war fought mostly on its own territory, Davis needed to remind his audience of the alternative had they not seceded or if they attempted to negotiate a return to the Union. According to Davis, the people of the Confederacy must "remember with devout thankfulness that it is to their own vigilance in resisting the first stealthy progress of approaching despotism that they owe their escape from consequences now apparent to the most skeptical."[27] The Emancipation Proclamation, according to Davis, should now convince the prewar skeptics that secession was a survival strategy for the slave states.

The Blessing and Curse of Confederate Conspiracy Discourse

Despite some important Confederate military victories in 1862, by January 1863 Jefferson Davis was in a difficult position as the leader of the Confederacy. The Confederate military strategy was struggling with the material advantages of a Union war machine that had more industry and more soldiers. Davis's response—the first draft on American soil—had triggered a political backlash, forcing him in his Mississippi address to utilize a strategy of amplification that described the Union as the ultimate enemy bent on destruction of the Confederacy. On January 1, 1863, however, the Emancipation Proclamation provided Davis a unique opportunity to shore up Confederate nationalism by reviving a set of conspiracy discourses that had helped propel the South into secession. In many ways, the Emancipation Proclamation was an ideal foil for Davis to rally Confederate nationalism. Rhetorical leadership, however, requires vision and an ability to assess the advantages and disadvantages of a particular rhetorical strategy. Davis's response to the Emancipation Proclamation demonstrates, once again, that he preferred to take advantage of short-term rhetorical gains regardless of the long-term consequences.

Nineteenth-century conspiracy discourse was a powerful tool that was wielded for tremendous political gain. As Michael William Pfau has noted, Chase, Sumner, and Lincoln owe much of their success in building the Republican Party to the "slave power" conspiracy that argued Southern slave owners were secretly controlling the highest ranks of the federal government.[28] Pfau articulates the power of conspiracy discourse in forming political parties and developing a sense of party commitment and loyalty.[29] Davis's response to the Emancipation Proclamation calls forth a similar set of rhetorical forces. Although Davis was not constituting a political party, he seized the rhetorical moment to isolate the Union as an unworthy enemy—dishonorable, committed to the total destruction of the Southern way of life, and willing to lie, cheat, and steal to achieve its nefarious aims. The power of these conspiracy discourses for Davis was their capacity to rekindle the passion of Toombs's original call for Southerners to take up arms and "throw the bloody spear into this den of incendiaries and assassins, and let God defend the right."

The Confederate response to Davis's revival of these powerful conspiracy discourses highlights the short-term success that can come from engaging in enemy creation through conspiracy discourse. The *Richmond Examiner*, which had demonstrated its willingness to attack Davis with fervor in the past, wrote on January 31, 1863, "The Republican party was formed, then, for the purpose of overthrowing the United States. Its aim was so to change the Constitution as to make it inimical to slavery. Beyond this it had no fixed party." The paper went on, "But in carrying out this new policy, in putting into practice the dogma of abolitionism, [Republicans have] found that an entirely new system of government must be adopted: a dictatorship which is fully upheld by the Republican party."[30] The *Raleigh (NC) Semi-Weekly Standard* repeated Davis's refrain that the Emancipation Proclamation "proves what were the designs of the Republican Party from the beginning, not-withstanding their efforts to conceal them by false declarations."[31]

Although the response throughout the Confederacy demonstrated the power of Davis's conspiracy discourse, the best evidence of its rhetorical force stems from the Northern politicians and pro-Union newspapers which grew anxious at the persuasiveness of Davis's argument. While speaking in opposition to the Union deploying black soldiers, Rep. George H. Pendleton of Ohio argued that Davis "seeks to justify the action of the confederate States in seceding from the Union. He seeks still further 'to fire the southern heart' and to unite the southern people. How? . . . He cites the action of the Administration itself, the acts of the President and the majority in both Houses of Congress. . . . These were the basis of his appeals to continued and persistent resistance. These, he said, were the fulfillment of his prophecies of what the Republican party would do when it had the power."[32] Pendelton was conscientious of the power of conspiracy discourse and Davis's ability to deploy it to build Confederate nationalism.

The *New York Herald* went further than Pendelton to argue that Davis's speech was especially dangerous, because it not only inspired Confederate nationalism but it also enflamed the controversy within the Union over the Emancipation Proclamation threatening to unite white people in the North against Lincoln: "The message of Jeff. Davis to the Confederate Congress is of more than ordinary importance. . . . It is true that the Confederate President is aware of the divisions and disgust at the North produced by the abolition policy, and particularly the emancipation edict extorted from Mr. Lincoln, which is worth two hundred thousand men to the cause of the rebellion; for it enables the rebel government to prove that their anticipations of the designs of the radical party are fully realized, and to make out a plausible case of justification before the people for the rebellion of the South. . . . The administration and the radicals seem to have given him a chance to appeal to the sympathies of the white men of the North and the Caucasian race throughout the world."[33] For Davis, the power in reviving these pre-secession conspiracy discourses was in the post hoc absolutist language that presented the inevitability of an abolitionist dictatorship. Every day that the Confederacy kept its independence, then, was a day of freedom in the fight between good and evil. An additional benefit of rekindling these pre-secession conspiracy discourses was their policy implications. As McPherson notes, Davis had been pressured into some version of negotiation on a handful of occasions throughout the war.[34] Alexander Stephens and other prominent members of the Confederacy consistently pressured Davis to help secure peace by allowing a small contingent of commissioners to approach their friends in the Union. Davis consistently argued that negotiation would be pointless, because Lincoln would demand reintegration with the Union and later complete abolition, but he acquiesced on more than one occasion.[35] After this address, however, there were fewer options for a negotiated peace.

Toombs's original pro-secession discourse established the impossibility of negotiating with an untrustworthy enemy. That had been a crucial argument in his public debate with Stephens and a key reason why Stephen's refusal to engage the merits of the conspiracy theory made his appeal to a reasoned institutional response less persuasive. Davis's speech cemented this foundational assumption that there were only two possible outcomes: independence or total defeat. Lincoln and the Union, in this understanding, were so untrustworthy that any negotiation would be brokering a deal with the Devil. The *North Carolina Standard*, which had been pushing for negotiations, saw the implications: "We regret to perceive that the President is still disposed to thrust his particular and ultra secessionist views upon the country."[36] There would be no room for treating the Union as a worthy adversary that could be negotiated with in good faith.

There were, however, dangers in wielding conspiracy discourse to achieve pragmatic aims. The return to the pro-secession conspiracy discourse reconstituted the Confederate identity's intimate tie to slavery. Although the Emancipation Proclamation met great resistance throughout the Union, the unilateral action set in motion a reconfiguration of the relationship between the United States and slavery. At that crucial moment, Davis chose to rhetorically reinvest in the institution of slavery. While he may not have seen that rhetorical investment as constraining in the moment, within a matter of months he would be asking the Confederate people to agree to sacrifice their rigid views on the institution of slavery in an effort to sustain the Confederate war effort.

The next chapter examines how Davis justified his desperate proposal for conditional emancipation, but it was his decision to re-center Confederate identity on preserving the institution of slavery—standing rhetorically alongside the fire-eaters and their radical conspiracy discourse—that marked his subsequent call for conditional emancipation as the end of Confederate nationalism.

5

Pragmatism and Desperation in Davis's Push for Conditional Emancipation

"Should the alternative ever be presented of subjugation or of the employment of the slave as a soldier, there seems no reason to doubt what should then be our decision."

—Jefferson Davis, *Jefferson Davis, Constitutionalist, Letters, Papers, and Speeches*

In the two years following Davis's response to the Emancipation Proclamation, the Confederate States of America suffered major setbacks in its campaign for independence. Despite Davis's controversial conscription policies, the Confederacy put 850,000 soldiers into the field compared to the Union's 2,100,000. By 1864, the Union was reaping the benefits of war industrialization including increased iron production, a burgeoning firearms industry, and astounding increases in overall manufacturing.[1] The South, by contrast, was suffering from devastating resource shortages and reaping the consequences of a war fought mostly on its own territory. Union invasions had destroyed almost all Southern industry, killed one-quarter of southern white men and two-fifths of Southern livestock, demolished half the machinery for Southern agriculture, and rendered thousands of miles of railroad useless.[2]

With military resources dwindling and Atlanta in enemy hands, Davis issued a message to the Confederate Congress on November 7, 1864. Tenuously balanced between assertions of victory and explanations for defeat, the message was steeped in the languages of desperation and hope. Throughout forty-one paragraphs, Davis addressed the status of the Confederate fight for independence in a speech that would be published and circulated throughout the North and the South. He dedicated the majority of his message to the status of the military campaigns in the east and west, foreign relations with England and France, finances, reorganization of the Department of War, negotiations for peace, and the "Employment of Slaves."[3]

Although Davis's message covered a wide variety of topics, the section on the "Employment of Slaves" demonstrates just how desperate the Confederate war effort was by this point in Davis's era of rhetorical leadership. In this section, Davis proposed "a radical modification in the theory of the law" through a policy of conditional emancipation that would grant freedom to 40,000 slaves if they helped to secure a Confederate victory through faithful service to the Confederate military effort. Given the significance of slavery and states' rights for the foundation of the Confederacy, this November 1864 address is an important window into the final moments of Davis's rhetorical leadership.

From his initial speeches as president to this moment of eminent collapse, Davis struggled to balance the pragmatic demands of war with his vision of Confederate nationalism based on principles contrary to a centralized war effort. At this moment in November 1864, Davis's proposal for conditional emancipation signaled the end of this struggle. He was no longer willing to make overtures to any principle that would place slavery, states' rights, or individual property over the survival of the Confederacy. The fundamental problem for Davis, however, was that his decision to focus on the survival of the Confederacy over anything else begged a series of difficult questions: what was the Confederacy apart from the institution of slavery? What was the ethos of the Confederacy without respect for states' rights? What was left that was worth fighting for, much less dying for? While it may have been too late for Davis to construct a new identity for the Confederacy at this moment of complete collapse, Davis's November 1864 address once again foregrounded independence for independence's sake at the expense of the rhetorical work to constitute a new meaning for the war effort. Without a new framework for interpreting the tremendous sacrifices of an extended war effort, Davis left his audience with little faith in the *idea* of the Confederacy.

Desperation in the Final Days of the Confederacy

Davis's November 1864 address was not the first time that conditional emancipation had been proposed in the Confederacy. Many of these earlier proposals, detailed by Robert F. Durden and Bruce Levine, came from the Confederate Army.[4] One of the most powerful proposals came from Patrick Cleburne of the Army of Tennessee.[5] On January 2, 1864, Cleburne wrote a memorandum that included one major general, three brigadier generals, four colonels, two lieutenant colonels, one captain, and one major wherein the officers pushed for emancipation if the slaves would fight for the Confederacy. The officers argued that there was a simple military necessity: "The immediate effect of the emancipation and enrollment of negroes on the military strength of the South would be: To enable us to have armies numerically superior to those of the North, and a reserve of any size we might think necessary; to enable us to take the offensive, move forward, and forage on the enemy."[6]

Importantly, the officers went beyond the straightforward argument about the need for more soldiers and into the more complicated realm of emancipation's symbolic nature. According to the memorandum, the move "would instantly remove all the vulnerability, embarrassment, and inherent weakness which result from slavery."[7] The officers went so far as to suggest that the move would damage the Union will to fight while bolstering Confederate nationalism. They wrote, "The very magnitude of the sacrifice itself, such as no nation has ever voluntarily made before, would appal [*sic*] our enemies, destroy his spirit and his finances, and fill our hearts with a pride and singleness of purpose which would clothe us with new strength in battle."[8] Cleburne's proposal for change, however, did not reach the public or the Confederate Congress.

The official policy of the Confederacy until November 1864 was to use slaves solely for support positions such as cooking, building fortifications, and manual labor.[9] The problem was that by 1864, the numbers of white soldiers that the Confederacy could count on to fight was quickly dwindling and the slaves were becoming force multipliers for the Union. When northern armies drew near to Confederate cities or armies, slaves would escape and provide intelligence to the Union. Cleburne's memo demonstrates that the shrinking numbers of soldiers and the Union's use of slaves as spies and soldiers was a severe problem. According to Levine, by 1863, Cleburne's army was battling 5,500 black soldiers from Arkansas and over 20,000 black soldiers from Tennessee.[10] Cleburne argued, "Every soldier in our army already knows and feels our numerical inferiority to the enemy. . . . Our single source of supply is that portion of our white men fit for duty and not now in the ranks."[11] He continued, "All along the lines slavery is comparatively valueless to us for labor, but of great and increasing worth to the enemy for information. It is an omnipresent spy system, pointing out our valuable men to the enemy, revealing secretly that there is no means to guard against it."[12] Despite support from key military figures for conditional emancipation, any proposal to include slaves in the Confederate Army faced almost insurmountable rhetorical obstacles as slavery and states' rights had been cornerstones in the creation of the Confederacy. Davis was so worried about the prospect of a newspapers securing a copy of Cleburne's memo that he ordered all copies of it destroyed. As McPherson notes, Davis's order was followed so carefully that "Cleburne's paper remained unknown outside of a small circle until 1890, when a copy saved by a member of Cleburne's staff turned up during the publication of the official records of the war."[13]

The relationship between the institution of slavery and the creation of the Confederacy demonstrates just how desperate Davis was in proposing conditional emancipation. The Confederacy had clearly designated black people as mentally, physically, and spiritually unfit for citizenry. In his response to the Emancipation Proclamation, Davis had emphasized the wisdom of secession as the only way to protect the institution of slavery from Lincoln's abolitionist agenda. From this perspective, any potential threat to slavery was treated as a threat to the Southern way of life that had served as the core value justifying secession. According to Thomas, "If the South seceded and went to war to defend her way of life against threats real and imagined, surely the 'peculiar institution' was the most threatened portion of Southernism, and thus in this context the 'cause' of the Civil War."[14] The relationship of slavery to the creation of the Confederacy was outlined in no uncertain terms by Vice President Alexander Stephens on March 21, 1861, when he declared, "Our new government is founded upon exactly the opposite idea; its foundations are laid, its cornerstone rests upon the great truth, that the negro is not equal to the white man; that slavery—subordination to the superior race—is his natural and normal condition."[15] The cornerstone of the Confederacy, according to Stephens, was the Confederacy's recognition of the legitimacy of the institution of slavery and the inferiority of black people.

Conditional emancipation also struck at a second cornerstone of the public justification for secession—states' rights. Any congressional mandate for conditional emancipation would necessitate a violation of states' rights at a time when there was deep discontent among the governors of the Confederacy at the prosecution of the war effort. Slaves, considered private property, were under the purview of the individual states. The *Charleston Mercury* published a staff editorial that summarized this argument on November 3, 1864: "Now, if there was any single proposition that we thought was unquestionable in the Confederacy it was this—that the States, and the States alone, have the *exclusive* jurisdiction and mastery over their slaves."[16] It continued, "To suppose that any slaveholding country (i.e., state) would voluntarily leave it to any other power than its own, to emancipate its slaves, is such an absurdity, that we do not believe a single intelligent man in the Confederacy could entertain it."[17] Davis's proposal would require the exercise of national power over the states on *the* most important public justification for secession—the potential for a national policy resulting in emancipation. As Thomas summarizes, "Southern politicians had raised the doctrine of state rights to the level of an article of faith. And as such, state rights seemed to some Southerners the very cornerstone of their way of life."[18] Any proposal for conditional emancipation would require Davis to undermine, if not destroy, the two central cornerstones that had served as justifications for the creation of the Confederacy.

Beyond the rhetorical obstacles stemming from the proposal itself, Davis confronted an additional problem—his own credibility, his ethos, had been shattered through a series of controversial wartime decisions and the overall state of the war effort. Historian William Davis argues, "By the winter of 1864–1865 certainly no one needed a clairvoyant to sense that the South was all but on its knees. The war appeared to start well . . . but numbers and resources and time all worked against Jefferson Davis and his cause."[19] As the South's vision of complete independence began to slip away, Davis's war policies came under attack from prominent Confederate voices including Vice President Alexander Stephens, Robert Toombs, Robert Barnwell Rhett, Gen. P. G. T. Beauregard, and Gen. Joseph Johnston.[20] Stephens was convinced that Confederate states needed to exert more independence to resist Davis's policies, while others advocated more radical solutions including an open call from Rhett to overthrow Davis and install Robert E. Lee as leader.[21] Toombs, who also advocated violence to overthrow Davis, summarized the opposition's position when he roared, "Begone Davis!"[22]

Rhetorical Strategies for Legitimation

With his nation collapsing and his military resources dwindling, Jefferson Davis proposed a radical change in the way the Confederacy prosecuted the war, which, in turn, represented a radical change in the content of the character of the Confederacy. The change required sacrificing the two core values that constituted the Confederate national identity at a time when his credibility as commander in chief was dwindling. Although the proposal was surely unthinkable at the outset of the war, desperation drove Davis to ask the Confederate Congress to authorize the conditional emancipation of slaves willing to fight for the Confederacy. This wartime proposal confronted tremendous rhetorical obstacles to achieve the legitimation it would need from the people, the military, and the rest of the Confederate government.

The goal of gaining legitimation for presidential actions is an important element of Karlyn Kohrs Campbell and Kathleen Hall Jamieson's analysis of war rhetoric. They argue that what "is central to war rhetoric [is] the need for the public and the Congress to legitimize presidential use of war powers for an end that has been justified. Each war message has this legitimation as its central persuasive purpose."[23] For Campbell and

Jamieson, legitimation is intimately tied to a president's attempt at gaining consent to use the powers of commander in chief to prosecute a war. In an effort to gain legitimation for his policy of conditional emancipation, Davis employed three rhetorical strategies. First, in a move similar to his defense of conscription, Davis carefully constructed a narrative of military operations that established his credibility as a wartime leader while simultaneously isolating troop resources as the central impediment to future Confederate victories.[24] Second, Davis constructed his audience as the persecuted chosen people in order to frame the meaning of the past Confederate military losses. Finally, Davis used his audience's unanimity of purpose to propose his radical policy change.

Davis began his quest for legitimation by constructing a narrative of Confederate battles from the past year.[25] He began by dividing the Confederacy along the Mississippi river into the West and the East. In the West, he argued that Texas, Louisiana, Arkansas, and Missouri had all been sites of large Confederate military successes. He proclaimed, "Our forces have penetrated into central Missouri, affording to our oppressed brethren in that State an opportunity . . . of striking for liberation from the tyranny to which they have been subjected."[26] Davis was just as exuberant about the status of Confederate forces in the East. Again he listed the Confederate victories in Alabama, Mississippi, and Tennessee. Davis's use of the broad geographic markers "West" and "East" ensured that everyone in the Confederacy could celebrate the military successes. Davis's narrative of Confederate victories restored his credibility because, according to the narrative, the Confederacy was winning crucial battles and he was orchestrating the charge.[27]

Although Davis's explanation of Confederate victories was clear and concise, a closer examination of the narrative reveals a more nuanced argumentative structure. Davis's narrative was tenuously balanced between assertions of victory and explanations for defeat. Within this balance, the difference between victory and defeat was the resource that Davis would later ask for—soldiers. Davis utilized the soldier argument through a similar pattern found in his Jackson, Mississippi, address on conscription. The inductive argument that Davis used from the beginning of the message was that the number of soldiers on the field dictated Confederate chances. Davis continually emphasized the overwhelming force of the Union to prepare his audience for the introduction of his plan for conditional emancipation. Davis characterized the conflict in terms of resources and soldiers early in the message when he described the status of the Union and Confederate war efforts. When describing the Union, Davis sounded in awe of "the magnitude of the preparations made by the enemy, the number of his forces, [and] the accumulation of his warlike supplies." In contrast, the Confederacy, Davis argued, deserved to be applauded for its successes given "the numbers and means at our disposal for resistance." Davis continued to develop a pattern of description that emphasized the number of soldiers for both Union and Confederate armies. For instance, when describing three separate battles, Davis put a primacy on the size of the armies involved: "in northwestern Louisiana a large and well-appointed army"; "the enemy hoped to effect during the present year, by concentration of forces"; and "after constant repulse of repeated assaults on our defensive lines, is, with the aid of heavy reinforcements."[28] In these three examples, Davis used the number of soldiers available for assaults, defensive lines, and reinforcements to paint a picture of valiant Confederate forces overrun by a sea of Union soldiers. Davis's references to the numbers of soldiers involved in battles remains consistent throughout his narrative of the Confederate victories and losses.

In order to further his argument for conditional emancipation, Davis needed to place the Confederacy in a delicate position. On the one hand, he needed his audience to agree that the South could still win independence with sufficient troop resources. On the other hand, Davis needed to dismiss other, less radical solutions to the resource disparity. Davis carefully constructed a narrative where the recent Confederate victories were the result of the honor and brilliance of the Confederate soldiers while highlighting that the army was quickly running out of those soldiers. Despite his exultation of Confederate victories, Davis was faced with a significant rhetorical problem that is unique to the advanced stages of a conflict—his side had lost major battles and faced the very real prospect of defeat. In order for his narrative to remain cohesive, Davis needed to create a framework of meaning for the recent military losses. In other words, Davis needed an explanation for why the Confederacy was losing that did not paint a picture of inevitability. For this, Davis turned to his second rhetorical strategy of constructing his audience as the persecuted chosen people whose dedication and faith in the cause were essential to their salvation.

As is the case with many rhetorics of desperation, religion played a critical role in Davis's message. In his earlier addresses, Davis relied on the civic republican notions of virtue to defend his policies. In his November 1864 address Davis redefined virtue through the frame of religion. He began by reiterating his amplification of Northern evil and Southern heroism, which constituted the North as an evil enemy willing to pour all its resources into ensuring the destruction of the South. This opening portion of Davis's speech was closely related to Campbell and Jamieson's description of the narrative forms in war rhetoric that justify initiating a military response to an evil opponent.[29] However, as Davis attempted to reconcile the recent military losses, the distinction between the initial stages of a conflict and the advanced stages of a conflict becomes clearer.

Instead of using "strategic misrepresentations" to dismiss the claims that the Union had a strategic advantage over the Confederacy, Davis used the continued survival of the Confederacy in the face of the Union's resource advantage as evidence of divine intervention.[30] Unlike his Jackson address, Davis embraced the vast resources of the Union and highlighted the structural disadvantages of the Confederacy. Although this introduction would seem problematic for leaders attempting to gain legitimacy from their people, Davis used the Union's overwhelming advantage to demonstrate that the South was truly God's chosen people—a rhetorical frame that was a new focus in Davis's later wartime addresses.

He began by examining the Union's strength. Davis once again asked his audience to consider "the magnitude of the preparations made by the enemy, the number of his forces, the accumulation of his warlike supplies, and the prodigality with which his vast resources have been lavished in the attempt to render success assured" and then compared the Union's resources to the Confederacy: "When we contrast the numbers and means at our disposal for resistance, and when we contemplate the results of a struggle apparently so unequal, we cannot fail . . . to perceive that a power higher than man has willed our deliverance." He concluded that the people should be grateful "to recognize the protection of a kind Providence in enabling us successfully to withstand the utmost efforts of the enemy for our subjugation."[31] Davis used the persistence of his audience as evidence of God's intervention. Their continuing existence demonstrated a divine intervention because they still lived outside the control of the Union. However, Davis again pointed to the Union's troop advantage as a way of cautioning his audience. In Davis's narrative, the enemy would continually pour troops onto the battlefield in an effort to conquer the South. Divine intervention had helped them survive on fewer resources, but it was up to the people of the South to ensure that they were doing all that they could to sacrifice for the cause. At some point, they must recognize that God helps those who help themselves.

Davis also used the wisdom of God to frame the recent Confederate losses. He once again began by emphasizing how much more powerful the Union armies have been in comparison to the Confederate armies. He proclaimed, "If we now turn to the results accomplished by the two great armies, so confidently relied on by the invaders as sufficient to secure the subversion of our Government and the subjugation of our people to foreign domination, we have still greater cause for devout gratitude to Divine Power."[32] Davis's introduction ensured that the audience was always considering how much worse things could have been as he addressed the specific instances of Union victories.

The capture of Atlanta was front and center in Davis's message. He argued, "The army of General Sherman, although succeeding at the end of the summer in obtaining possession of Atlanta, has been unable to secure any ultimate advantage from this success." Davis continued, "The same general, who in February last marched a large army from Vicksburg to Meridian with no other result than being forced to march back again, was able, by the aid of greatly increased numbers and after much delay, to force a passage from Chattanooga to Atlanta."[33] Davis did not simply call the army a Union army but instead personalized the discussion by naming General Sherman, constituting the general as a metonymy for the Union at large. According to Davis, without divine wisdom, General Sherman was a military failure. Davis turned to Sherman's personal history to emphasize this point. He argued that Sherman had a history of powerful armies but lacked the wisdom to know what to do with them. Davis suggested that it was the sheer number of Sherman's troops that led to Atlanta's fall, but that it took Sherman a long time to capture such a defenseless city. Davis used Sherman as an example of the ignorant leaders of the Union who stood in stark contrast to the brilliance of the Confederacy's military leaders like Robert E. Lee. In doing so, Davis was able to frame the Confederate losses as a result of brute power and not brilliant strategy.

In explaining Sherman's lack of wisdom, Davis made the transition from discussing Atlanta to discussing all of the Confederate cities that could be captured. He argued, "The lessons afforded by the history of this war are fraught with instruction and encouragement. Repeatedly during the war have formidable expeditions been directed by the enemy against points ignorantly supposed to be of a vital importance to the Confederacy."[34] Davis argued that there were no cities that the Union could capture that would break the Confederacy, a refrain that he would return to in his final address in the desperation of losing Richmond. For now, the people of the Confederacy were the chosen people, which meant they should continue to fight for their divine right to independence. Davis's narrative was now complete: the only structural disadvantage inhibiting Confederate independence was the sheer magnitude of the Union armies, and he had a proposal for that very problem.

Davis Proposes Emancipation

Davis's section on conditional emancipation was entitled "Employment of Slaves." In this section, Davis asked the Confederate Congress to conscript forty thousand slaves and train them to fight for the Confederacy. If the slaves were loyal to the Confederate war effort, they would be rewarded with their freedom. Given the tremendous sacrifice that his proposal required, Davis could not merely rely on his earlier inductive argument and narrative. In this section Davis spoke directly to the states' rights and proslavery advocates who would surely oppose his proposal.

Davis began by reviewing the various roles assigned to slaves in the Confederate war effort. He reminded the audience that the Confederate Congress had already conscripted twenty-thousand slaves for use in noncombat positions. After establishing that a legal precedent had already been set for the Confederate government to conscript slaves into service for the war effort, Davis proposed his "radical modification in the theory of the law."[35] In order to circumvent the states' rights argument, Davis proposed that slaves had two distinct relationships to any governing institution. The first relationship was that of property. Davis had already established that the Confederate government had the power to confiscate property if it was necessary for the war effort. He acknowledged that this was traditionally a states' rights domain but that the exigency of war required the ability of the Confederacy to trump states' rights to ensure the adequate provision of resources.

The second relationship involved the connection that *all* people had to their governing institutions. He argued, "The slave, however, bears another relation to the State—that of a person. The law of last February contemplates only the relation of the slave to the master and limits the impressment to a certain term of service."[36] In this move, Davis asserted that the slaves were not only property but also people who could aid in the war effort. The distinction is critical because as property, slaves could be conscripted to the war and ultimately returned to their slave owners. To arm the slaves and ask them to fight as soldiers with the promise of their freedom required Davis to acknowledge a set of mental, physical, and spiritual capabilities that had been dismissed in order to substantiate the oppressive system of slavery. As soldiers, slaves would by definition be capable of acting valiantly, achieving honor, and ultimately dying for the Confederate war effort. Acknowledging both the potential of slaves to do these honorable things and the inevitable change that it would bring to the status of slaves throughout the Confederacy required Davis to present a strong argument for the Confederate government's ability to conscript the "personhood" of the slaves over the states' rights to maintain them solely as property, restricted in role and to be returned at the conclusion of the war.

Davis immediately argued that the "personhood" of slaves was more important than their status as property: "In this respect the relation of person predominates so far as to render it doubtful whether the private right of property can consistently and beneficially be continued, and it would seem proper to acquire for the public service the entire property in the labor of the slave."[37] Although Davis quickly argued that the slave owners would be fully compensated for their loss of property, Davis proposed that the war effort was ultimately more important than individual's property and states' rights, because the need for the slaves' "personhood" was more beneficial to the Confederacy than their status as property.

Davis's justification for emancipation centered on the need for loyalty among soldiers, which is a distinctly human quality, but one that had been deployed in racist ways throughout the history of slavery. Davis used loyalty to answer the argument that the slaves could be conscripted to fight without giving them their freedom, relegating them to their antebellum roles at the conclusion of the war. He argued, "The permission would doubtless be more readily accorded as a reward for past faithful service . . . their freedom and the gratification of the local attachment which is so marked a characteristic of the negro, and forms so powerful an incentive to his action." Davis continued, "The policy of engaging to liberate the negro on his discharge after service seems to me preferable to that of granting immediate manumission, or that of retaining him in servitude."[38] Davis thus used a long held racial stereotype to justify conditional emancipation. He argued that "local attachment" was a characteristic of slaves that made them more willing to fight for the Confederacy if they were offered their freedom and the ability to stay in the South. He attempted to assuage the fears of immediate emancipation by arguing that faithful execution of duties would be a condition of freedom. The condition helped Davis answer the argument that simply serving in the Confederate Army would be a path to equality. According to Davis, slaves would never be equal to white people; however, if they were willing to die for the Confederacy then they should be given the opportunity to fight for their freedom and rewarded with it if they helped the Confederacy achieve independence.

After setting out his legal precedent for conscription, Davis turned to his last rhetorical strategy—establishing a unanimity of purpose to justify radical actions. According to Campbell and Jamieson, the unanimity of purpose is an essential feature of war rhetoric as leaders move their audience to be willing to make tremendous sacrifices in the name of the greater cause. They argue, "Presidential war rhetoric constitutes the audience as a united community of patriots that is urged to repulse the existing threat with all available resources, assured that with the help of Providence, right will prevail."[39] In Davis's case, the question was whether or not the audience would agree to use "all available resources" in the name of fighting the Union. Davis attempted to situate himself in the middle of the debate by arguing that slaves should only be used when the Confederate resources were in dire straits. As we saw earlier, Davis constructed his audience as the persecuted chosen people who *were* willing to make any sacrifices to achieve independence. Davis used their unanimity of purpose to preserve the Confederacy as a trump card against other values. He used a worst case scenario to argue that "should the alternative ever be presented of subjugation or of the employment of the slave as a soldier, there seems no reason to doubt what should then be our decision." He continued, "The appalling demoralization, suffering, disease, and death which have been caused by partially substituting the invader's system of police for the kind relation previously subsisting between the master and slave have been a sufficient demonstration that external interference with our institution of domestic slavery is productive of evil only."[40] Davis used the unanimity of purpose to establish that everyone in the Confederacy, facing an exceptional threat, should be willing to make the necessary sacrifices for the independence.

Rhetorical Leadership at the Threshold of Defeat

Jefferson Davis's message to the Confederate Congress on November 7, 1864, offers unique insights into his struggles as a rhetorical leader on the brink of destruction. There is little room for debate: Davis's push for conditional emancipation was an act of total desperation. His message eviscerated the institution of slavery and the states rights' doctrine, the twin cornerstones of Confederate identity. Recognizing his nearly impossible task, Davis's November 1864 address reveals some of the more impressive rhetorical strategies he deployed as President of the Confederacy. He utilized narrative and inductive argument to legitimize conditional emancipation through a ruthless adherence to pragmatism and a creative interpretation of the legal powers of the Confederate government. With the public support of Robert E. Lee, Davis garnered the legitimacy his proposal needed.[41] The Confederate Congress recognized the desperate state of affairs and authorized Jefferson Davis to recruit up to three hundred thousand slaves to fight for the Confederacy.[42] Some slaves were immediately recruited, put into companies, and even paraded through Southern cities, but much to Robert E. Lee's chagrin the war ended before they were put into official service.[43] One of Lee's last memos to Davis, dated April 2, 1865, explained that Lee was so desperate that he was "willing to detach officers to recruit negro troops" in order to speed up the process.[44]

Not surprisingly, several newspaper editorials opposed conditional emancipation on the grounds that it would threaten the core of Southern society and would result in complete equality for African Americans. The newspaper the *Republican* summarized this position on November 2, 1864, stating, "If the negro is made to fight our battles of 'freedom' then he must be governed by the same laws of war, and he must stand upon the same footing of the white man after the war." The editorial clarified, "In other words, the South is to be converted by this war into an abolitionized colony of free negroes, instead of a land of white freemen. . . . If they are to be armed like the master, then they *are in fact* equal to the master."[45] Other editorials argued that the Confederacy seceded in order to preserve slavery and, therefore, to emancipate the slaves would make the fight meaningless. An editorial published in the *Enquirer*, for instance, argued, "What has embittered the feelings of the two sections of the old Union? What has gradually driven them to the final separation? What is it that has made two nationalities of them, if it is not slavery?" The editorial continued, "It was slavery that caused them to denounce us [as] inferiors; it was slavery that made the difference in our Congressional representatives; it was slavery which made the difference in our pursuits, in our interests. . . . It is slavery which now makes of us two people, as widely antagonistic and diverse as any two people can be."[46] The editorial established the link between slavery and separate national identities. Since the seventeenth century, the South had a special relationship to slavery. By the 1860s, the maintenance and expansion of the institution of slavery was the central reason that the South needed its own nation. Some papers went so far as to continue to defend slavery as a positive good that the slaves should be willing to fight for without any promise of emancipation, "If the slave must fight, he should fight for the blessings he enjoys as a slave, and not for the miseries that would attend him if freed."[47]

As impressive as Davis's justification for conditional emancipation was, the newspaper responses highlight that it also represented the final blow to any notion of Confederate nationalism. As was the case throughout his term as rhetorical leader, Davis utilized rhetorical strategies to achieve a short-term pragmatic victory without reconciling the damage that those rhetorical choices were doing to the foundation of Confederate nationalism. Until this point in the war, he had been able to make those sacrifices with some hope that he could restore Confederate nationalism when the fledgling nation had finally achieved peace and independence. With this last rhetorical victory, however, no longer could he point to the wisdom of secession in preserving slavery and states' rights.

Several historians point to conditional emancipation as an indication not only that the Confederacy was on the verge of military defeat but that the concept of the Confederacy itself had all but vanished. Thomas points to conditional emancipation to substantiate his argument that by the end the Confederacy sacrificed everything it purportedly had seceded to protect. He argues, "Faced with choosing between independence and the Southern way of life, the Confederacy chose independence. . . . The fact was that the Confederacy was prepared to let slavery perish and to fight on! For what?" Thomas surmises that the decision to sacrifice the institution of slavery signaled the official change from the Confederacy using secession to preserve Southern values to the Confederacy sacrificing Southern values to preserve secession. He argues, "In four years the Southern nation had given up that which called it into being. Independence at last was no longer means but end. . . . Had the heavens opened, the waters parted, and the Confederacy achieved independence, the postwar South would have resembled the prewar South in little more than name."[48] Escott makes the final connection between nationalism and the collapse of the Confederacy: "Internal dissensions seriously weakened the Confederacy, for there is a clear link between the failure of Jefferson Davis to build a spirit of Confederate nationalism at home and the inability of southern generals to establish Confederate independence on the battlefield."[49] In the end, Davis was not rhetorically competent enough to sustain the Confederacy, because he did not articulate a vision of the imagined community without slavery and states' rights. Although pragmatically effective, Davis's November 1864 address was more about what was missing than what was present. Davis needed to offer a new vision of the Confederacy without the institution of slavery. This was his rhetorical failure.

We point to Abraham Lincoln's Gettysburg Address as a defining point in US history, when our national identity was constructed.[50] At Gettysburg, instead of focusing on policies to increase the Union war effort, Lincoln used 272 words to construct an identity that Americans hold onto today. Davis had no equivalent to the Gettysburg address. Over his tenure, the Confederacy's imagined community became synonymous with independence for independence's sake, offering no larger purpose for soldiers, officials, and the Confederate people as they made the greatest sacrifices in memory.

Conclusion

Six months after Davis's desperate call for conditional emancipation, the Confederacy was on the brink of losing its capital at Richmond, Virginia. By April 3, 1865, the Confederate government was on the move as Grant's forces were poised to capture the city that had been at the center of the Eastern Theater of war for close to four years. Davis escaped to Danville, Virginia, where the next day he issued his last official address as president of the Confederacy. It was only five paragraphs long, and in it Davis embraced the defiant, if not delusional, optimism that had become a hallmark of his late wartime addresses. Although the address did little to persuade anyone to press on, it does represent a final answer to the questions: what was Davis willing to give up in the name of independence, and what would the Confederacy stand for without states' rights and the institution of slavery? Based on his last address as president, the answers are everything and nothing.

Rather than admitting that the loss of Richmond foretold the imminent collapse of the Confederacy, Davis argued that the event was a crucial military blunder by the Union that would only improve the chances of a Confederate victory in its bid for independence as the pride of the Confederacy, Robert E. Lee, would now finally be free to attack wherever he wished without the burden of protecting the Confederate capital.[1] Davis's weak argument relied on redefining victory and defeat so that the only path to Union victory was to break Confederate will to fight in every instance. Ironically, according to Davis, as long as there was a strong sense of Confederate nationalism then the Confederacy itself would live on regardless of what cities were occupied and what capitals were lost.[2] Davis's call, then, was for the Confederate people to demonstrate their resolve by continuing to support the war effort despite losing Richmond. According to Davis, this collective act of defiance would not only have tangible military benefits but would likely break the will of the Northern people to continue fighting in the face of such strong Confederate nationalism.

The problem for Davis was that, even if his audience agreed that nationalism was the standard of victory, there was little Confederate nationalism left. The people of the Confederacy had sacrificed so much to the pragmatic demands of war that the call to fight on was an empty call to a vanquished audience. Davis's rhetorical options were limited, and his final speech demonstrates that when nationalism was all that was left, Davis still did not have a vision for the Confederacy outside of the well-trodden claims of independence in the face of a fierce enemy. After losing states' rights, the institution of slavery, territory, and now the capital of the Confederacy, there was simply nothing left to fight for.

Davis's final address represents a series of mistakes that culminated in his struggles as a rhetorical leader. First, Davis took his audience's unwavering commitment to the Confederacy for granted from start to finish. Throughout his interpersonal fights and his public addresses, one theme that seemingly infuriated Davis more than any other was opposition to his policies grounded in purely sectional interest. Early in the war, Davis was constantly asking governors for more troops to address problems outside their states; nothing angered him more than resistance to those requests in the name of state interest. For Davis, the decision to secede may have been made on a state-by-state basis, but after the Montgomery convention his life's mission became the independence of the Confederacy as a whole. He assumed that everyone else would be just as motivated to achieve that goal; often he demanded it. The record reflects that Davis's commitment to "all for one and one for all" was shared in the early days when resources were plentiful, battles had not been fought, and the Union was not occupying large swaths of territory. As resources grew tighter and difficult decisions had to be made, people could not help but act on sectional interest. As the war progressed toward total devastation and Davis orchestrated a military strategy that ceded large portions of the Confederacy in order to concentrate forces in critical areas, people could not help but think that they had been abandoned.

For many, Davis's final address must have been a tough pill to swallow. He proclaimed that the loss of Richmond was actually good, because "for many months the largest and finest army of the Confederacy, under the command of a leader whose presence inspires equal confidence in the troops and the people, has been greatly trammeled by the necessity of keeping constant watch over the approaches to the capital, and thus been forced to forego more than one opportunity for promising enterprise."[3] If Lee's efforts to defend Richmond had in fact kept him from more promising enterprise, it left the audience to question why Davis had not abandoned Richmond far earlier? Davis had conscripted troops far beyond the borders of Virginia in the name of protecting Richmond. Now, on the precipice of defeat, Davis was declaring that those lives lost in the name of protecting the capital city were not only lost in vain but perhaps represented a flawed military objective from the start. Thus, in his last moments as rhetorical leader, Davis added insult to death. From his perspective, the unwavering support of his audience should lead them to the same conclusion: there were always new battles to fight. For the families of Confederate dead in shallow graves throughout the Eastern Theater, however, Davis's thought experiment did little to encourage continued war.

Davis's second mistake was once again investing his rhetoric in short-term goals. At the rhetorical birth of the Confederacy, Davis had done an excellent job of marshaling the rhetorical traditions of the past to support the core tenets of the new Confederate nation. His Senate resignation and presidential inauguration reveal a man well-versed in the civic republican tradition, using it to constitute the Confederacy as the true heirs of the American Revolution, peaceful farmers toiling away with little want of war, committed to states' rights, and willing to protect their "domestic" institutions from any foreign interference or moral judgment. That constitutive rhetoric was powerful, inspiring, and exactly the type of statesmanship that put Davis in the position of rhetorical leader instead of Robert Toombs. Then, the cannons started firing.

As soon as the first shots were fired, the content and the character of the Confederacy changed. Farmers would not win this war. Wars require industrialization, concentration of resources, material sacrifices, and an inevitable centralization of power and decision-making that is inconsistent with the states' rights doctrine that sounded so appealing to the Montgomery audience for his first inaugural. Davis, however, refused to articulate for his people how the Confederacy was changing, let alone offer a vision of what it should become. Perhaps he was too close to it. Perhaps his refusal to delegate left him wading through papers rather than realizing that his wartime decisions were inconsistent with the nation he had helped introduce to the world in the wake of secession. Either way, Davis bounced from controversy to controversy rousing public sentiment and arguing that defeating such a fierce, evil, and committed enemy required the Confederate people to match them with a greater commitment, since it would not be possible to match them soldier to soldier.

Each rhetorical victory set the stage, ultimately, for a final rhetorical defeat. He won the fight for conscription, which took away one of the core tenets of states' rights. He succeeded in attacking the Emancipation

Proclamation by reestablishing the connection between the Confederate identity and the institution of slavery, which doomed his later efforts to articulate a Confederate identity that could sustain conditional emancipation. He then won the fight for conditional emancipation at the expense of the two cornerstones of states' rights and the institution of slavery. At each turn, he used rhetorical maneuvers that positioned the Confederacy as one sacrifice away from independence. As losses mounted, resources dwindled, and Confederate troops disappeared from camps to go home, Davis kept reaching into his rhetorical arsenal and finding less and less to offer. In his last address, Davis asked his audience to sacrifice whatever territory, city, or capital was necessary to keep fighting. Thus, Davis proposed sacrificing the last vestige of Confederate identity—its geographic markers that separated it from the Union.

Some argue that Davis's fierce commitment to sacrifice shows an unwavering commitment to the Confederacy. That may be true, but as a rhetorical leader, that is only half of the equation. Davis needed to step forward and offer his audience a new vision of what the Confederacy stood for. What were the principles that were now uncompromising? What goals was the nation seeking? It would appear that Davis would answer each of these with: independence. The problem, of course, was that independence alone does little to inspire nationalism when, in practice, the Confederacy had sacrificed so many of the concepts that made it independent from the Union in the first place. This was the rhetorical legacy Jefferson Davis took with him in his escape from Richmond.

After the war, Davis's two years in prison awaiting trial were no match for the public backlash he endured. Leaders of losing sides are rarely treated differently no matter how excellent their orations. But with his eulogy at Lee's funeral in 1870, Davis began to restore his image throughout the South. In his eulogy he shielded Lee from blame for the Confederate defeat and helped sow the seeds of the "lost cause" narrative which reestablished honor for the Confederate dead. Davis's eulogy for Lee and his infamous book, *The Rise and Fall of the Confederate Government*, published a little over a decade later, demonstrate Davis's awareness of the need for rhetorical leadership *after* the war.[4] In retrospect he had no problems helping reconstitute the honor of the Confederate identity by moving it away from the institution of slavery. At his boldest moment he asserted, "The truth remains intact and incontrovertible, that the existence of African servitude was in no wise the cause of the conflict, but only an incident." One need look no farther than Davis's own response to the Emancipation Proclamation to see that this was an impossible interpretation of the role of slavery in secession. The very words he had used to rally Confederate nationalism and diminish the prospects for negotiated peace in 1863 celebrated secession as the *only* way to protect slavery. Davis's post hoc attempt to reconstruct Confederate identity was impossible given his own addresses to inspire nationalism throughout the war.

The only people today who take Davis's post hoc explanations seriously are neo-Confederates unwilling to read Davis's own words throughout the war. His attempt does show, however, his lack of vision for the Confederacy during the war: when he realized the implications of his rhetorical choices later, that he had led a rebellion forged in and committed to one of the greatest atrocities in our nation's history, he fought a vigorous retreat. He attempted to use his powers of persuasion to rewrite the history of the Confederacy—to create a vision of the nation that would grant the Confederate dead some honor rather than leave them martyrs to slavery. Davis's effort after the war to step back into his role as rhetorical leader, to erase his own words, and to redefine the Confederacy suggests the rhetorical regrets he carried. However he rationalized it, he had come in some way to agree with this book's hypothesis: that President Jefferson Davis struggled in his role as rhetorical leader for the Confederacy.

Notes

Introduction

1. James McPherson, *Embattled Rebel: Jefferson Davis as Commander in Chief* (New York: Penguin Press, 2014), 206, 225.

2. Benedict Anderson, *Imagined Communities: Reflections on the Origins and Spread of Nationalism* (London: Verso Editions and NLB, 1983).

3. Emory M. Thomas, *The Confederacy as a Revolutionary Experience* (Columbia: University of South Carolina Press, 1991), 131.

4. Garry Wills, *Lincoln at Gettysburg: The Words that Remade America* (New York: Simon & Schuster, 1992), 130.

5. David Zarefsky, "Consistency and Change in Lincoln's Rhetoric About Equality," *Rhetoric & Public Affairs* 1 (1998): 39-40.

6. Frank Alfriend, *The Life of Jefferson Davis* (Chicago: Caxton Publishing House, 1868); Varina Davis, *Jefferson Davis: Ex-President of the Confederate States of America: A Memoir by His Wife* (New York: Bedford Co., 1890); William Dodd, *Jefferson Davis* (Philadelphia: G. W. Jacobs, 1907); Dunbar Rowland, *Jefferson Davis's Place in History: As Revealed in His Letters, Papers, and Speeches* (Jackson: Torgeson Press, 1923); Clement Eaton, *Jefferson Davis* (New York: Free Press, 1977); Cass Canfield, *The Iron Will of Jefferson Davis* (New York: Fairfax Press, 1978); Steven Woodworth, *Jefferson Davis and His Generals: The Failure of Confederate Command in the West* (Lawrence: University Press of Kansas, 1990); William C. Davis, *Jefferson Davis: The Man and His Hour* (New York: Harper Collins Pub., 1991); Felicity Allen, *Jefferson Davis: Unconquerable Heart* (Columbia: University of Missouri Press, 1999); William J. Cooper Jr., *Jefferson Davis, American* (New York: Alfred Knopf, 2000); Herman Hattaway and Richard Beringer, *Jefferson Davis, Confederate President* (Lawrence: University Press of Kansas, 2002); William J. Cooper Jr., *Jefferson Davis and the Civil War Era* (Baton Rouge: Louisiana State University Press, 2008); James McPherson, *Embattled Rebel: Jefferson Davis as Commander in Chief* (New York: Penguin Press, 2014).

7. McPherson, *Embattled Rebel*, 111.

8. John Russell Bartlett, *The Literature Of The Rebellion: A Catalogue Of Books And Pamphlets Relating To The Civil War In The United States, And On Subjects Growing Out Of That Event, Together With Works on American Slavery, And Essays from Reviews and Magazines on the Same Subjects* (Boston: Draper and Halliday, 1866); Richard E. Beringer et al., *Why the South Lost the Civil War* (Athens: University of Georgia Press, 1986); Brian Dirck, *Lincoln and Davis: Imagining America, 1809–1865* (Lawrence: University Press of Kansas, 2001); *Inside the Confederate Nation: Essays in Honor of Emory Thomas*, ed. Lesley Gordon and John Inscoe (Baton Rouge: Louisiana State University Press, 2005); Emory Thomas, *The Confederate Nation, 1861–1865* (New York, Harper & Row, 1979); Emory Thomas, *The Confederacy as a Revolutionary Experience* (Columbia: South Carolina Press, 1991); Frank Vandiver, *Jefferson Davis and the Confederate State* (New York: Oxford University Press, 1964); Richard Bensel, *Yankee Leviathan: The Origins of Central State Authority in America, 1859–1877* (Cambridge: Harvard University Press, 1991); Raimondo Luraghi, "The Civil War and the Modernization of American Society," Civil War History 28 (1972): 230–50, Paul Escott, *After Secession: Jefferson Davis and the Failure of Confederate Nationalism* (Baton Rouge: Louisiana State University Press, 1978); Drew Gilpin Faust, *The Creation of Confederate Nationalism: Ideology and Identity in the Civil War South* (Baton Rouge: Louisiana State University Press, 1982); G. S. Boritt and James M. McPherson, *Why The Confederacy Lost* (New York: Oxford University Press, 1992).

9. Paul Escott, *After Secession: Jefferson Davis and the Failure of Confederate Nationalism* (Baton Rouge: Louisiana State University Press, 1978), xii.

Chapter 1

1. Hudson Strode, *Jefferson Davis: Private Letters 1823–1889* (New York: Da Capo Press, 1995), 120.

2. Jefferson Davis, Lynda Crist, and Mary Dix, *The Papers of Jefferson Davis* (Baton Rouge: Louisiana State University Press, 1992), 23.

3. Clement Eaton, *Jefferson Davis* (New York: Collier Macmillan Publishers, 1977), 109.

4. Ibid.

5. William J. Cooper Jr., *Jefferson Davis, American* (New York: Alfred A. Knopf, 2000), 314.

6. Jefferson Davis to Robert Barnwell Rhett Jr., Nov. 10, 1860, *The Papers of Jefferson Davis*, vol. 6, ed. Lynda Crist and Mary Dix (Baton Rouge: Louisiana State University Press, 1989), 368–70.

7. William C. Davis, *Jefferson Davis: The Man and His Hour* (New York: Harper Collins Publishers, 1991), 287.

8. Ibid.

9. Buchanan initially agreed with Davis's suggestions but later changed the address, making Davis's early trip back to Washington meaningless.

10. Cooper Jr., *Jefferson Davis*, 317.

11. Davis, *Jefferson Davis*, 288.

12. Jefferson Davis, *The Congressional Globe*, 2nd Session 36th Congress (1860–1861): 12.

13. Jefferson Davis, "To Our Constituents," *The Papers of Jefferson Davis*, vol. 6, ed. Lynda Crist and Mary Dix (Baton Rouge: Louisiana State University Press, 1989), 368–70.

14. Jefferson Davis, *The Congressional Globe*, 2nd Session 36th Congress (1860–1861): 29.

15. Ibid., 29.

16. As quoted in Robert McElroy, *Jefferson Davis: The Unreal and the Real* (New York: Harper & Brothers Publishers, 1937), 234–35.

17. Cooper Jr., *Jefferson Davis*, 319.

18. Ibid., 319–20.

19. Davis, *The Rise and Fall of the Confederate Government*, 199.

20. Jefferson Davis to J. J. Pettus, Jan. 4, 1861, *Jefferson Davis Constitutionalist: His Letters, Papers, and Speeches*, vol. 4, ed. Dunbar Rowland (Jackson: Mississippi Department of Archives and History, 1923), 564–65.

21. Jefferson Davis to Edwin De Leon, Jan. 8, 1861, *The Papers of Jefferson Davis*, vol. 7, ed. Lynda Crist and Mary Dix (Baton Rouge: Louisiana State University Press, 1992), 6–7.

22. Davis, *The Rise and Fall of the Confederate Government*, 58.

23. Jefferson Davis to J. J. Pettus, Jan. 4, 1861, *Jefferson Davis Constitutionalist*, 564–65.

24. Robert R. Potter, *Jefferson Davis* (Austin, Tex.: Raintree Steck-Vaughn, 1994), 74; Felicity Allen, *Jefferson Davis, Unconquerable Heart* (Columbia: University of Missouri Press, 1999), 197–98.

25. Eaton, *Jefferson Davis*, 122.

26. Varina Davis, *Jefferson Davis: Ex-President Of The Confederate States Of America; A Memoir By His Wife*, vol. 1 (New York: Belford, 1890), 696–97.

27. Ibid., 697.

28. Clement Clay, "Resignation," *The Congressional Globe*, 2nd Session 36th Congress (1860–1861), 486.

29. Robert Toombs, "Resignation," *The Congressional Globe*, 2nd Session 36th Congress (1860–1861), 267.

30. Ibid., 267.

31. Ibid.

32. *New York Times*, March 1, 1860; James Jasinski, *Sourcebook on Rhetoric: Key Concepts in Contemporary Rhetorical Studies* (Thousand Oaks, CA: Sage Publications, Inc., 2001), 147; Cicero, Orator, 357–59.

33. Marcus Tullius Cicero, Brutus. *Orator*, G. L. Hendrickson and H. M. Hubbell Trans. (Cambridge, MA: Harvard University Press, 1939).

34. Michael Leff, "Decorum and Rhetorical Interpretation: The Latin Humanistic Tradition and Contemporary Critical Theory," *Vichiana* 1, 3a Series, (1990): 107–26.

35. See Janet Atwill, *Rhetoric Reclaimed: Aristotle and the Liberal Arts Tradition* (Ithaca, NY: Cornell University Press, 1998); Elaine Fantham, "Orator 69–74," *Central States Speech Journal* 35 (1984): 123–25; Fantham, *The Roman World of Cicero's De Oratore* (New York: Oxford University Press, 2004).

36. Leff, "Decorum and Rhetorical Interpretation," 112.

37. Ibid.

38. See Thomas Rosteck and Michael Leff, "Piety, Propriety, and Perspective: An Interpretation and application of key terms in Kenneth Burke's Permanence and Change," *Western Journal of Speech Communication* (1989): 332; John Poulakos, "Toward a Sophistic Definition of Rhetoric," *Philosophy & Rhetoric* 16 (1983): 35–48; Michael Mendelson, *Many Sides: A Protagorean Approach to the Theory, Practice and Pedagogy of Argument* (Boston: Kluwer Academic Publishers, 2002), 237.

39. Leff, "Decorum and Rhetorical Interpretation," 121.

40. Jasinski, *Sourcebook on Rhetoric*, 149.

41. Robert Hariman, "Decorum, Power, and the Courtly Style," *Quarterly Journal of Speech* 78 (1992): 155.

42. Crist, *The Papers of Jefferson Davis*, 16.

43. Quoted in Clement Eaton, *Jefferson Davis*, 112.

44. Jefferson Davis, "Speech of Resignation," *Congressional Globe*, January 21, 1861, 487.

45. Celeste Condit, "The Functions of Epideictic: The Boston Massacre Orations as Exemplar," *Communication Quarterly* 33 (1985): 284–99.

46. Condit, "The Functions of Epideictic."

47. Davis, "Speech of Resignation," 487.

48. Condit, "The Functions of Epideictic," 289.

49. Ibid., 288.

50. Ibid.

51. Davis, "Speech of Resignation," 487.

52. Celeste Condit, "The Functions of Epideictic," 289.

53. Davis, "Speech of Resignation," 487.

54. Ibid.

55. Ibid.

56. Ibid

57. Ibid.

58. Bruce Gronbeck, "Rhetorical Timing in Public Communication," *Central States Speech Journal* 25 (1974): 84.

59. For a detailed description of the history of kairos as a concept, see the introduction to Phillip Sipiora and James Baumlin, *Rhetoric and Kairos: Essays in History, Theory, and Praxis* (Albany: State University of New York Press, 2002), 1–22.

60. Atwill, *Rhetoric Reclaimed*, 57.

61. Ibid.

62. In the prologue to Walter Jost and Michael Hyde's *Rhetoric and Hermeneutics in Our Time: A Reader* (New Haven, CT: Yale University Press, 1997), the authors argue that kairos "remains beyond the control of the rhetor, coming rather as a gift or even magic (goetia). In short, the emphasis falls on kairos as receptivity" (xv).

63. John Poulakos, "Toward a Sophistic Definition of Rhetoric," *Philosophy & Rhetoric* 16 (1983): 35–48.

64. Poulakos, "Toward a Sophistic Definition of Rhetoric," 41–42.

65. Ibid.

66. Crist, *The Papers of Jefferson Davis*, 16.

67. Jefferson Davis to Francis Perkins, Jan. 13, 1861, *Jefferson Davis Constitutionalist: His Letters, Papers, and Speeches*, vol. 5, ed. Dunbar Rowland (Jackson: Mississippi Department of Archives and History, 1923), 37.

68. Jefferson Davis to George Jones, Jan. 20, 1861, *Jefferson Davis Constitutionalist: His Letters, Papers, and Speeches*, vol. 5, ed. Dunbar Rowland (Jackson: Mississippi Department of Archives and History, 1923), 39.

69. Davis, *The Rise and Fall of the Confederate Government*, 57.

70. Eaton, *Jefferson Davis*, 83.

71. Ibid.

72. *Ibid.*, 84.

73. Davis, *The Rise and Fall of the Confederate Government*, 57–58.

74. Davis, "Speech of Resignation," 487.

75. Ibid.

76. *Daily Exchange*, January 22, 1861, no. 894, pg. 1

77. Varina Davis, *Jefferson Davis*, 698.

78. *Charleston Mercury*, "Our Washington Correspondence," January 26, 1861.

79. Abraham Lincoln, "First Inaugural Address," *Messages and Papers of the Presidents*, ed. James Daniel Richardson (New York: New York Bureau of National Literature, Inc., 1897).

80. Garry Wills, *Lincoln at Gettysburg: The Words That Remade America* (New York: Simon & Schuster, 1992).

Chapter 2

1. Emory Thomas, *The Confederate Nation: 1861–1865* (New York: Harper & Row, 1979), 62.

2. William C. Davis, *Jefferson Davis: The Man and His Hour* (New York: Harper Collins Publishers, 1991), 310.

3. Jefferson Davis to John Callan, Feb. 7, 1861, *The Papers of Jefferson Davis*, vol. 7, ed. Lynda Crist and Mary Dix, (Baton Rouge: Louisiana State University Press, 1992), 52–53.

4. South Carolina, Mississippi, Alabama, Louisiana, Florida, and Georgia

were present throughout the entire convention. Texas was the only state that held a public referendum on secession and, as a result, was delayed in coming to Montgomery.

5. Thomas, *The Confederate Nation*, 43.

6. William Cooper Jr., *Jefferson Davis, American* (New York: Alfred A. Knopf, 2000), 326.

7. Jefferson Davis to Alexander Clayton, Jan. 30. 1861, *The Papers of Jefferson Davis*, vol. 7, ed. Lynda Crist and Mary Dix (Baton Rouge: Louisiana State University Press, 1992), 27.

8. "The Southern Confederacy," *New Orleans Daily Crescent*, February 20, 1861.

9. Varina Davis, *Jefferson Davis: Ex-President of the Confederate States of America: A Memoir by his Wife*, vol. II (New York: Belford Company Publishers, 1890), 18–19.

10. Herman Hattaway and Richard Beringer, *Jefferson Davis: Confederate President* (Lawrence: University Press of Kansas, 2002), 19.

11. Emory Thomas, *The Confederacy as a Revolutionary Experience* (Columbia: University of South Carolina Press, 1971), 38–39.

12. Ibid.

13. Thomas, *The Confederate Nation*, 37.

14. Issac Kramnick, *Republicanism and Bourgeois Radicalism: Political Ideology in Late Eighteenth Century England and America* (Ithaca: Cornell University Press, 1990), 1.

15. See Gordon Wood, *The Creation of the American Republic: 1776–1787* (Chapel Hill: University of North Carolina Press, 1969); Bernard Bailyn, *The Ideological Origins of the American Revolution* (Cambridge: Belknap Press of Harvard University Press, 1967); J. G. A. Pocock, *Politics, Language, and Time: Essays on Political Thought and History* (New York: Atheneum, 1972).

16. Wood, *The Creation of the American Republic*, 47.

17. Stephen Browne, "Arts of Address in Revolutionary America," Andrea Lundsford, ed., *Sage Handbook of Rhetoric* (Thousand Oakes, CA: Sage Publications, 2009): 230–45; Stephen Hartnett and Jennifer Mercieca, "'Has Your Courage Rusted?': National Security and The Contested Rhetorical Norms of Republicanism in Post-Revolutionary America, 1798–1801," *Rhetoric & Public Affairs* 9 (2006): 79; James Jasinski, "Instrumentalism, Contextualism, and Interpretation in Rhetorical Criticism," in *Rhetorical Hermeneutics: Invention and Interpretation in the Age of Science*, ed. Alan G. Gross and William M. Keith (Albany: State University of New York Press, 1997), 197; James Jasinski, "Beyond the Intentionalist Paradigm: Further Thoughts on Context as Performative Tradition," National Communication Association Convention, Chicago, IL, November, 1997; James Jasinski, "History, Theory, and Thinness: Notes on Recovering the Performative Traditions in American Public Address," Speech Communication Association Convention, San Antonio, TX, November, 1995; James Jasinski, "The Forms and Limits of Pru-

dence in Henry Clay's (1850) Defense of the Compromise Measures," *Quarterly Journal of Speech* 81 (1995): 455; Jennifer Mercieca, *Founding Fictions* (Tuscaloosa, University of Alabama Press, 2010); John Murphy, "Intervening Authority: Bill Clinton, Martin Luther King, Jr., and the Orchestration of Rhetorical Traditions," *Quarterly Journal of Speech* 83 (1997): 71.

18. Gordon Wood, *The Radicalism of the American Revolution* (New York: Alfred A. Knopf, 1992), 104.

19. John Murphy, "Civic Republicanism in the Modern Age: Adlai Stevenson in the 1952 Presidential Campaign," *Quarterly Journal of Speech*, 80, (1994): 314.

20. Wood, *The Creation of the American Republic*, 56.

21. Ibid., 55.

22. Ibid., 59.

23. Murphy, "Civic Republicanism in the Modern Age," 315.

24. Ibid.

25. Ibid., 316.

26. Davis, *Jefferson Davis*, 302.

27. Ibid.

28. Ibid., 303.

29. Hattaway and Beringer, *Jefferson Davis*, 20.

30. Ibid., 19.

31. Wood, *The Creation of the American Republic*, 69.

32. Robert Toombs, Milledgeville, November 13, 1860.

33. Jefferson Davis to Alex Clayton, Jan. 30. *The Papers of Jefferson Davis*, vol. 7, ed. Lynda Crist and Mary Dix (Baton Rouge: Louisiana State University Press, 1992), 27–28.

34. Wood, *The Creation of the American Republic*, 68.

35. Karyln Kohrs Campbell and Kathleen Hall Jamieson, *Deeds Done in Words: Presidential Rhetoric and the Genres of Governance* (Chicago: University of Chicago Press, 1990), 14.

36. Thomas Cobb, quoted in William C. Davis, *Jefferson Davis: The Man and His Hour*, 303.

37. Jefferson Davis, "Inaugural Address," *The Papers of Jefferson Davis*, vol. 7, ed. Lynda Crist and Mary Dix (Baton Rouge: Louisiana State University Press, 1992), 46.

38. James R. Andrews, "Oaths Registered in Heaven: Rhetorical and Historical Legitimacy in the Inaugural Addresses of Jefferson Davis and Abraham Lincoln," *Doing Rhetorical History: Concepts and Cases*, ed. Kathleen J. Turner (Tuscaloosa: University of Alabama Press, 1998), 107.

39. Murphy, "Civic Republicanism in the Modern Age," 315.

40. Ibid.

41. Thomas, *The Confederacy As A Revolutionary Experience*, 7.

42. Jefferson Davis, "Inaugural Address," 46–47.

43. Davis, *Jefferson Davis*, 308.

44. James Read, *Power versus Liberty: Madison, Hamilton, Wilson, and Jefferson* (Charlottesville: University Press of Virginia, 2000), 145.

45. Jefferson Davis, "Inaugural Address," 49.

46. Davis, *Jefferson Davis*, 308.

47. Abraham Lincoln, "Inaugural Address," *The Collected Works of Abraham Lincoln,* ed. Roy Basler (New Brunswick, NJ: Rutgers University Press, 1953), 267.

48. Ibid., 268.

49. Read, *Power versus Liberty*, 121.

50. Murphy, "Civic Republicanism in the Modern Age," 326.

51. Ibid.

52. Davis, "Inaugural Address," 46.

53. Kramnick, *Republicanism and Bourgeois Radicalism*, 275.

54. Davis, "Inaugural Address," 47–48.

55. Drew McCoy, *The Elusive Republic: Political Economy in Jeffersonian America* (Chapel Hill: University of North Carolina Press, 1980), 237.

56. Davis, "Inaugural Address," 46.

57. Ibid.

58. Stephen Browne, "'The Circle of Our Felicities': Thomas Jefferson's First Inaugural Address and the Rhetoric of Nationhood," *Rhetoric and Public Affairs,* vol. 5 no.3 (2002), 432.

59. "Inauguration of President Davis," *Richmond Daily Dispatch*, February 19, 1861.

60. "The News," *Baltimore Daily Exchange*, February 19, 1861.

61. Davis, *Jefferson Davis*, 410.

62. Louis Wigfall to Jefferson Davis, Feb. 18, 1861, *The Papers of Jefferson Davis*, vol. 7, ed. Lynda Crist and Mary Dix (Baton Rouge: Louisiana State University Press, 1992), 51.

63. Beverly Tucker to Jefferson Davis, Mar. 20, 1862, *The Papers of Jefferson Davis,* vol. 8, ed. Lynda Crist and Mary Dix (Baton Rouge: Louisiana State University Press, 1995), 108–9.

64. "President's Inaugural," *Edgefield (SC) Advertiser*, February 27, 1861.

65. "From Montgomery, Ala.," *Daily Nashville Patriot*, February 19, 1861.

66. "The Southern Confederacy," *New Orleans Daily Crescent*, February 20, 1861.

67. "Inaugural of President Davis," *Anderson (SC) Intelligencer*, February 28, 1861.

Chapter 3

1. John Pettus to Jefferson Davis, Dec. 1, 1862, *The Papers of Jefferson Davis*, vol. 8, ed. Lynda Crist and Mary Dix, (Baton Rouge: Louisiana State University Press, 1995), 525.

2. Crist and Dix, *The Papers of Jefferson Davis*, 565.

3. William C. Davis, *Jefferson Davis: The Man and His Hour* (New York: Harper Collins Publishers, 1991), 485.

4. "Speech of President Davis to the Legislature of Mississippi, Dec. 26," *Western Democrat*, January 13, 1863.

5. Albert Moore, *Conscription and Conflict in the Confederacy* (Atlanta: MacMillan Company, 1924), 5.

6. Davis, *Jefferson Davis*, 454.

7. Davis, *Jefferson Davis*, 454; Albert Sidney Johnston was a close friend of Jefferson Davis who considered him one of the Confederacy's best generals. He was killed at the battle of Shiloh.

8. Emory Thomas, *The Confederate Nation: 1861–1865* (New York: Harper & Row, 1979), 165.

9. Moore, *Conscription and Conflict in the Confederacy*, 4.

10. Ibid.

11. Ibid., 6.

12. Emory Thomas, *The Confederacy as a Revolutionary Experience* (Columbia: University of South Carolina Press, 1971), 61.

13. Ibid., 60.

14. Earl Hess, *Pickett's Charge—The Last Attack at Gettysburg* (Chapel Hill: University of North Carolina Press, 2001).

15. Michael Fellman, Lesley Gordon, and Daniel Sutherland, *This Terrible War: The Civil War and Its Aftermath* (New York: Pearson Education, 2003).

16. Thomas, *The Confederacy as a Revolutionary Experience*, 61.

17. Clement Eaton, *Jefferson Davis* (New York: MacMillan Publishing Co, Inc., 1977), 141.

18. Moore, *Conscription and Conflict in the Confederacy*, 12.

19. Ibid.

20. Ibid., 7.

21. Ibid., 8–9.

22. Jefferson Davis, Message to the Confederate Congress, Mar. 28, 1862, *The Messages and Papers of Jefferson Davis and the Confederacy: Including Diplomatic Correspondence 1861–1865*, vol. 1, ed. James Richardson (New York: R. R. Bowker, 1966), 205–6.

23. Moore, *Conscription and Conflict in the Confederacy*, 14.

24. Thomas, *The Confederate Nation*, 155.

25. Herman Hattaway and Richard Beringer, *Jefferson Davis: Confederate President* (Lawrence: University Press of Kansas, 2002), 162.

26. Moore, *Conscription and Conflict in the Confederacy*, 26.

27. Davis, *Jefferson Davis*, 436.

28. William Cooper Jr., *Jefferson Davis, American* (New York: Alfred A. Knopf, 2000), 384.

29. Davis, *Speech at Jackson, Mississippi*, 565.

30. Ibid., 566.

31. John M. Murphy, "Our Mission and Our Moment: George W. Bush and September 11th" *Rhetoric and Public Affairs* 6.4 (2003), 609.

32. Robert L. Ivie, "Images of Savagery in American Justifications for War," *Communication Monographs* 47 (1980): 279–94.

33. Davis, *Jefferson Davis*, 488.

34. Richard Lanham, *A Handlist of Rhetorical Terms* (Berkeley: University of California Press, 1991), 26.

35. Kenneth Burke, *A Rhetoric of Motives* (Berkeley: University of California Press, 1969), 69.

36. Giambattista Vico, *The Art of Rhetoric: Institutiones Oratoriae, 1711–1741*, trans. Giorgio Pinton and Arthur Shippee (Atlanta: Rodopi, 1984), 95.

37. Davis, *Speech at Jackson, Mississippi*, 566.

38. Ibid.

39. Ibid.

40. Ibid.

41. Ibid.

42. Ibid.

43. Ibid.

44. Chaïm Perelman and L. Olbrechts-Tyteca, *The New Rhetoric: A Treatise on Argumentation*, trans. John Wilkinson and Purcell Weaver (Notre Dame, IN: Notre Dame University Press, 1969), 116.

45. Davis, *Speech at Jackson, Mississippi*, 566.

46. Ibid.

47. Ibid.

48. Ibid.

49. Ibid.

50. See Campbell and Jamieson's discussion of strategic misrepresentation in their outline of the basic themes of war rhetoric in *Deeds Done in Words*.

51. Davis, *Speech at Jackson, Mississippi*, 566.

52. Ibid.

53. Ibid.

54. Ibid., 444.

55. Paul Escott, *After Secession: Jefferson Davis and the Failure of Confederate Nationalism* (Baton Rouge: Louisiana State University Press, 1978), 180.

56. Paul Escott, *After Secession*, 180.

57. Davis, *Speech at Jackson, Mississippi*, 566.

58. "Jeff. Davis's Jackson Speech—His Contempt for Non-Slaveholders," *Nashville Daily Union*, January 21, 1863.

59. "News," *Chattanooga Daily Rebel*, January 4, 1863.

60. *Richmond Examiner*, January 26, 1863.

61. "The Propositions of the Rebels," *Wheeling (VA) Daily Intelligencer*, January 16, 1863.

Chapter 4

1. Abraham Lincoln, *The Collected Works of Abraham Lincoln, Vol. 5*, ed. Roy Basler (New Brunswick, NJ: Rutgers University Press, 1953), 433–36.

2. See Harold Holzer, *Emancipating Lincoln: The Proclamation in Text, Context, and Memory* (Cambridge, MA: Harvard University Press, 2012); Kirt H. Wilson, "The Paradox of Lincoln's Rhetorical Leadership," *Rhetoric & Public Affairs* 3, no. 1 (Spring 2000): 15–32; David Zarefsky, "Consistency and Change in Lincoln's Rhetoric about Equality," *Rhetoric & Public Affairs* 1 (1998): 21–44.

3. Lincoln, *The Collected Works of Abraham Lincoln*, 28–30.

4. William Freehling and Craig Simpson, *Secession Debated: Georgia's Showdown in 1860* (New York: Oxford University Press, 1992), 46–47.

5. Freehling and Simpson, *Secession Debated*, 45–47.

6. Ibid., 47.

7. Ibid., 53.

8. Ibid., 54–56.

9. Ibid., 54.

10. Ibid., 56.

11. Ibid.

12. Ibid., 56–57.

13. Ibid., 56–58.

14. Richard Hofstadter, *The Paranoid Style in American Politics and Other Essays* (Cambridge, MA: Harvard University Press), 31.

15. John Inscoe, *The Civil War in Georgia* (Athens: University of Georgia Press, 2011), 38.

16. Davis, *Jefferson Davis*, 302.

17. Davis, *The Messages and Papers Of Jefferson Davis and The Confederacy*, 290.

18. James McPherson, *Embattled Rebel: Jefferson Davis as Commander in Chief* (New York: Penguin Press, 2014), 121.

19. Davis, *The Messages and Papers Of Jefferson Davis and The Confederacy*, 290.

20. "The Message of Jeff. Davis," *Cleveland Morning Leader*, January 17, 1863.

21. Davis, *The Messages and Papers Of Jefferson Davis and The Confederacy*, 290.

22. Ibid., 290–91.

23. Hofstadter, *The Paranoid Style in American Politics and Other Essays*, 35–36.

24. Davis, *The Messages and Papers Of Jefferson Davis and The Confederacy*, 291.

25. Ibid., 292.

26. Ibid.

27. Ibid.

28. Michael William Pfau, *The Political Style of Conspiracy: Chase, Sumner, and Lincoln* (East Lansing: Michigan State University Press, 2005).

29. Ibid.

30. John Daniel, "January 31, 1863," *The Richmond Examiner during the War* (New York: Printed for the author [Daniel], 1868), 68–69.

31. "Confederate Congress," *Raleigh (NC) Semi-Weekly Standard*, January 16, 1863.

32. "Speech of Hon. George H. Pendleton, of Ohio on the enlistment of Negro soldiers," Delivered to the House of Representatives, January 31, 1863.

33. "Message of Jeff. Davis—The Duty of Mr. Lincoln," *New York Herald*, January 17, 1863.

34. McPherson, *Embattled Rebel*, 202.

35. Ibid., 203.

36. *North Carolina Standard*, "Wednesday, January 31, 1863," 1.

Chapter 5

1. James M. McPherson, *Battle Cry of Freedom: The Civil War Era* (New York: Oxford University Press, 1988), 816–17.

2. McPherson, *Battle Cry of Freedom*, 818.

3. Davis, "Message to Congress," 102.

4. Robert Durden, *The Gray and the Black: The Confederate Debate on Emancipation* (Baton Rouge: Louisiana State University Press, 1972); Bruce Levin, *Confederate Emancipation: Southern Plans to Free and Arm Slaves During the Civil War* (New York: Oxford University Press, 2006).

5. According to Albert Castel, Cleburne was a widely respected and highly decorated officer. Castel argues that "Cleburne's words carry weight." Albert Castel, *Decision in the West: The Atlanta Campaign of 1864* (Lawrence: University of Kansas Press, 1992), 37.

6. Cleburne, "Commanding General, The Corps, Division, Brigade, and Regimental Commanders of the Army of Tennessee," 2 Jan. 1864, *The Gray and the Black: The Confederate Debate on Emancipation*, Ed. Richard Durden (Baton Rouge: Louisiana State University Press, 1972), 59.

7. Cleburne, "Commanding General, The Corps, Division, Brigade, and Regimental Commanders of the Army of Tennessee," 59.

8. Ibid., 60.

9. Levine, *Confederate Emancipation*, 72.

10. Ibid.

11. Cleburne, "Commanding General, The Corps, Division, Brigade, and Regimental Commanders of the Army of Tennessee," 56.

12. Ibid.

13. McPherson, *Embattled Rebel: Jefferson Davis as Commander in Chief* (New York: Penguin Press, 2014), 230.

14. Emory Thomas, *The Confederacy as a Revolutionary Experience* (Columbia: South Carolina Press, 1991), 10.

15. Alexander Stephens, March 25, 1861, quoted in *The Gray and the Black: The Confederate Debate on Emancipation*, 7–8.

16. *Charleston Mercury*, November 3, 1864, quoted in *The Gray and the Black: The Confederate Debate on Emancipation*, 97.

17. Ibid.

18. Thomas, *The Confederacy as a Revolutionary Experience*, 3.

19. William Davis, *An Honorable Defeat: The Last Days of the Confederate Government* (New York: Harcourt, Inc., 2001), 4.

20. Davis, *An Honorable Defeat*, 5.

21. Ibid.

22. Ibid.

23. Karlyn Kohrs Campbell and Kathleen Hall Jamieson, *Deeds Done in Words: Presidential Rhetoric and the Genres of Governance* (Chicago: University of Chicago Press, 1990), 101.

24. For a discussion of narrative theory see Walter Fisher, "Narration as Human Communication Paradigm: The Case of Public Moral Argument." in *Communication Monographs* 51 (1984), 1–22; Walter Fisher, "The Narrative Paradigm: An Elaboration," in *Communication Monographs* 52 (1985), 347–67; Walter Fisher, *Human Communication as Narration: Toward a Philosophy of Reason, Value, and Action* (Columbia: University of South Carolina Press, 1987).

25. Davis, "Message to Congress," 385.

26. Ibid.

27. Davis was not inaccurate in citing these victories, but the Confederacy still faced military defeat on a strategic scale. The explanation rests in Union military strategy, which was concerned with concentrating major forces against major Confederate armies. The Union was not attempting to occupy the entire South but instead to destroy the Confederacy's war-making capacity. As a result, the Confederacy reseized lands that the Union had once occupied but subsequently left. This strategy is summarized in Castel's discussion of the Meridian Mississippi Campaign. Castel argues that Sherman attacked Meridian and destroyed the railroads, repair shops, barracks, an arsenal, and a hospital. His attack was so efficient and surprising, however, that by the time the Confederate reinforcements arrived, Sherman had moved on. Much to Sherman's surprise, the newspapers reported the campaign as a victory for the Confederacy, because Sherman was unable to move from Meridian to Mobile or Montgomery. Castel, *Decision in the West*, 43–56.

28. Davis, "Message to Congress," 384.

29. Campbell and Jamieson, *Deeds Done in Words*, 107.

30. Campbell and Jamieson describe strategic deceptions as follows: "Presidential war rhetoric, however, evinces an unusual tendency to misrepresent the events described therein in ways strategically related to the president's desire to stifle dissent and unify the nation for immediate and sustained action," *Presidents Creating the Presidency: Deeds Done in Words* (Chicago: University of Chicago Press, 2008), 242.

31. Davis, "Message to Congress," 384.

32. Ibid., 386.

33. Ibid.

34. Ibid.

35. Ibid.

36. Ibid., 394.

37. Ibid., 395.

38. Ibid.

39. Campbell and Jamieson, *Presidents Creating the Presidency*, 231.

40. Davis, "Message to Congress," 396.

41. Durden, *The Gray and The Black*, 204–24.

42. Thomas, *The Confederacy as a Revolutionary Experience*, 130.

43. Ibid.

44. Robert E. Lee, "To Jefferson Davis," *The Wartime Papers of R. E. Lee* (Boston: Little, Brown, and Company, 1961), 927.

45. *The Republican*, "November 2, 1864," quoted in *The Gray and the Black: The Confederate Debate on Emancipation*, 94.

46. *Enquirer*, "November 4, 1864," quoted in *The Gray and the Black: the Confederate Debate on Emancipation*, 89–90.

47. "Jefferson Davis' Message," *Richmond Whig*, November 9, 1864.

48. Thomas, *The Confederacy as a Revolutionary Experience*, 131.

49. Escott, *After Secession*, xii.

50. Garry Wills, *Lincoln at Gettysburg: The Words that Remade America* (New York: Simon & Schuster, 1992), 130.

Conclusion

1. James Richardson and Allan Nevins, *The Messages and Papers Of Jefferson Davis and The Confederacy, Including Diplomatic Correspondence, 1861–1865*, Volume I (New York: Chelsea House–R. Hector, 1966), 569.

2. Davis, *The Messages and Papers Of Jefferson Davis and The Confederacy*, 569.

3. Ibid., 568.

4. Jefferson Davis, *The Rise and Fall of the Confederate Government*, vol. I, (New York: D. Appleton and Company, 1881), 53.

Bibliography

Alfriend, Frank H. *The Life of Jefferson Davis*. Cincinnati: Caxton Publishing House, 1868.

Allen, Felicity. *Jefferson Davis, Unconquerable Heart*. Columbia: University of Missouri Press, 1999.

Anderson, Benedict R. O'G. *Imagined Communities*. London: Verso, 1991.

Andrews, James. "Oaths Registered In Heaven: Rhetorical And Historical Legitimacy In The Inaugural Addresses Of Jefferson Davis And Abraham Lincoln." In *Doing Rhetorical History: Concepts and Cases*. (Studies in Rhetoric and Communications). Edited by Kathleen J. Turner, 95–117. Tuscaloosa: University of Alabama Press, 1998.

Atwill, Janet. *Rhetoric Reclaimed*. Ithaca, NY: Cornell University Press, 1998.

Bailyn, Bernard. *The Ideological Origins of the American Revolution*. Cambridge, MA: Belknap Press of Harvard University Press, 1967.

Bartlett, John R. *The Literature of the Rebellion*. Boston: Draper and Halliday, 1866.

Bensel, Richard F. *Yankee Leviathan*. Cambridge, UK: Cambridge University Press, 1990.

Beringer, Richard E., Herman Hattaway, Archer Jones, and William N. Still Jr. *Why the South Lost the Civil War*. Athens: University of Georgia Press, 1986.

Boritt, G. S., and James M McPherson. *Why the Confederacy Lost*. New York: Oxford University Press, 1992.

Browne, Stephen H. "The Circle of Our Felicities: Thomas Jefferson's First Inaugural Address and the Rhetoric of Nationhood." *Rhetoric & Public Affairs* 5, no. 3 (2002): 409–38.

———. "Arts of Address in Revolutionary America". In *Sage Handbook of Rhetoric*. Edited by Andrea Lundsford, 230–45. Thousand Oaks, CA: Sage Publications, 2009.

Burke, Kenneth. *A Rhetoric of Motives*. Berkeley: University of California Press, 1969.

Campbell, Karlyn Kohrs and Kathleen Hall Jamieson. *Deeds Done In Words*. Chicago: University of Chicago Press, 1990.

Canfield, Cass. *The Iron Will of Jefferson Davis*. New York: Fairfax Press, 1978.

Castel, Albert E. *Decision in the West*. Lawrence: University Press of Kansas, 1992.

Charleston Mercury. "Our Washington Correspondence," 1861.

Cicero, Marcus T., G. L. Hendrickson, and H. M. Hubbell. *Brutus. Orator*. Cambridge, MA: Harvard University Press, 1939.

Condit, Celeste M. "The Functions of Epideictic: The Boston Massacre Orations as Exemplar." *Communication Quarterly* 33, no. 4 (1985): 284–98.

Cooper, William J., Jr. *Jefferson Davis and the Civil War Era*. Baton Rouge: Louisiana State University Press, 2008.

———. *Jefferson Davis, American*. New York: Alfred A. Knopf, 2000.

Daily Dispatch. "Inauguration of President Davis," 1861.

Daily Exchange. "The News," 1861.

Daily Intelligencer. "The Propositions of the Rebels," 1863.

Daniel, John. *The Richmond Examiner during the War*. New York: Printed for the Author, 1868.

Davis, Jefferson. *The Rise and Fall of the Confederate Government*. New York: Appleton, 1881.

———. *Jefferson Davis, Constitutionalist*. Edited by Dunbar Rowland. Jackson, MS: Printed for the Mississippi Dept. of Archives and History, 1923.

———. *The Messages and Papers of Jefferson Davis and the Confederacy, Including Diplomatic Correspondence, 1861–1865*, vol. 1. Edited by James D Richardson. New York: Chelsea House–R. Hector, 1966.

———. *The Messages and Papers of Jefferson Davis and the Confederacy, Including Diplomatic Correspondence, 1861–1865*, vol. 2. Edited by James D Richardson. New York: Chelsea House–R. Hector, 1966.

———. *The Papers of Jefferson Davis*. Edited by Lynda L Crist and Mary S. Dix. Baton Rouge: Louisiana State Univ. Press, 1989.

———. *The Papers of Jefferson Davis*. Edited by Lynda L Crist and Mary S. Dix. Baton Rouge: Louisiana State University Press, 1992.

———. *Private Letters, 1823–1889*. Edited by Hudson Strode. New York: Da Capo Press, 1995.

Davis, Varina. *Jefferson Davis*. New York: Belford Company, 1890.

Davis, William C. *Jefferson Davis*. New York: HarperCollins, 1991.

Dirck, Brian R. *Lincoln & Davis*. Lawrence: University Press of Kansas, 2001.

Dodd, William E. *Jefferson Davis*. Lincoln: University of Nebraska Press, 1997.

Durden, Robert F. *The Gray and the Black: The Confederate Debate on Emancipation*. Baton Rouge: Louisiana State University Press, 1972.

Eaton, Clement. *Jefferson Davis*. New York: Free Press, 1977.

Edgefield Advertiser. "President's Inaugural," 1861.

Escott, Paul D. *After Secession*. Baton Rouge: Louisiana State University Press, 1978.

Fantham, Elaine. "Orator 69–74". *Central States Speech Journal* 35 (1984): 123–25.

———. *The Roman World of Cicero's De Oratore*. New York: Oxford University Press, 2004.

Faust, Drew Gilpin. *The Creation of Confederate Nationalism*. Baton Rouge: Louisiana State University Press, 1988.

Fellman, Michael, Lesley J Gordon, and Daniel E Sutherland. *This Terrible War*. New York: Longman, 2003.

Freehling, William W., and Craig M Simpson. *Secession Debated*. New York: Oxford University Press, 1992.

Gronbeck, Bruce E. "Rhetorical Timing in Public Communication." *Communication Studies* 25, no. 2 (1974): 84–94.

Hariman, Robert. "Decorum, Power, and the Courtly Style." *Quarterly Journal of Speech* 78, no. 2 (1992): 149–72.

Hartnett, Stephen J., and Jennifer Rose Mercieca. "'Has Your Courage Rusted?' National Security and the Contested Rhetorical Norms of Republicanism in Post-Revolutionary America, 1798–1801." *Rhetoric &Amp; Public Affairs* 9, no. 1 (2006): 79–112. doi:10.1353/rap.2006.0024.

Hattaway, Herman, and Richard E Beringer. *Jefferson Davis, Confederate President*. Lawrence: University Press of Kansas, 2002.

Hess, Earl J. *Pickett's Charge-The Last Attack at Gettysburg*. Chapel Hill: University of North Carolina Press, 2001.

Inscoe, John. *The Civil War in Georgia*. Athens: University of Georgia Press, 2011.

Ivie, Robert L. "Images of Savagery in American Justifications for War." *Communications Monographs* 47, no. 4 (1980): 279–94.

Jasinski, James. "Instrumentalism, Contextualism, and Interpretation in Rhetorical Criticism." In *Rhetorical Hermeneutics: Invention and Interpretation in the Age of Science*. Albany: State University of New York Press, 1997.

———. *Sourcebook on Rhetoric*. Thousand Oaks, CA: Sage Publications, 2001.

———. "The Forms and Limits of Prudence in Henry Clay's (1850) Defense of the Compromise Measures." *Quarterly Journal of Speech* 81, no. 4 (1995): 454–78.

Kramnick, Isaac. *Republicanism and Bourgeois Radicalism*. Ithaca: Cornell University Press, 1990.

Lanham, Richard A. *A Handlist of Rhetorical Terms*. Berkeley: University of California Press, 1991.

Lee, Robert E., and Clifford Dowdey. *The Wartime Papers of R. E. Lee*. Boston: Little, Brown, 1961.

Leff, Michael. "Decorum and Rhetorical Interpretation: The Latin Humanistic Tradition and Contemporary Critical Theory." *Vichiana* 1, no. 3 (1990): 107–26.

Levine, Bruce C. *Confederate Emancipation*. New York: Oxford University Press, 2006.

Lincoln, Abraham. *A Compilation of the Messages and Papers of the Presidents*. Edited by James D. Richardson. New York: Bureau of National Literature, 1897.

———. *The Collected Works of Abraham Lincoln*. Edited by Roy P Basler. New Brunswick, NJ: Rutgers University Press, 1953.

Luraghi, Raimondo. "The Civil War and the Modernization of American Society: Social Structure and Industrial Revolution in the Old South before and During the War". *Civil War History* 18, no. 3 (1972): 230–50. doi:10.1353/cwh.1972.0076.

McCoy, Drew R. *The Elusive Republic*. Chapel Hill: Published for the Institute of Early American History and Culture, Williamsburg, VA, by the University of North Carolina Press, 1980.

McElroy, Robert M. *Jefferson Davis; the Unreal and the Real*. New York: Harper & Bros., 1937.

McPherson, James M. *Battle Cry of Freedom*. New York: Oxford University Press, 1988.

———. *Embattled Rebel: Jefferson Davis as Commander In Chief*. New York: Penguin, 2014.

Mendelson, Michael. *Many Sides: A Protagorean Approach to the Theory, Practice and Pedagogy of Argument*. Dordrecht: Springer Netherlands, 2002.

Mercieca, Jennifer R. *Founding Fictions*. Tuscaloosa: University of Alabama Press, 2010.

Moore, Albert B. *Conscription and Conflict in the Confederacy*. New York: Macmillan Co., 1924.

Murphy, John M. "Our Mission and Our Moment: George W. Bush and September 11th." *Rhetoric & Public Affairs* 6, no. 4 (2003): 607–32.

———. "Inventing Authority: Bill Clinton, Martin Luther King, Jr., and the Orchestration of Rhetorical Traditions." *Quarterly Journal of Speech* 83, no. 1 (1997): 71–89. doi:10.1080/00335639709384172.

———. "Civic Republicanism in the Modern Age: Adlai Stevenson in the 1952 Presidential Campaign." *Quarterly Journal of Speech* 80, no. 3 (1994): 313–28.

Nashville Daily Union. "Jeff. Davis's Jackson Speech-His Contempt for Non-Slaveholders," 1863

New Orleans Daily Crescent. "The Southern Confederacy," 1861.

North Carolina Standard. "Wednesday, January 31, 1863," 1863.

Pendleton, George. "Speech of Hon. George H. Pendleton, Of Ohio on the Enlistment of Negro Soldiers, January 31." Speech, House of Representatives, 1863.

Perelman, Chaïm, Lucie Olbrechts-Tyteca, and Purcell Weaver. *The New Rhetoric*. Notre Dame: University of Notre Dame Press, 1971.

Pfau, Michael W. *The Political Style of Conspiracy*. East Lansing: Michigan State University Press, 2005.

Pocock, J. G. A. *Politics, Language and Time*. London: Methuen, 1972.

Potter, Robert R. *Jefferson Davis*. Austin, TX: Raintree Steck-Vaughn, 1994.

Poulakos, John. "Toward A Sophistic Definition of Rhetoric." *Philosophy & Rhetoric* 16, no. 1 (1983): 35–48.

Read, James H. *Power versus Liberty*. Charlottesville: University Press of Virginia, 2000.

Richmond Examiner, 1863.

Richmond Whig. "Jefferson Davis' Message," 1864.

Rosteck, Thomas, and Michael Leff. "Piety, Propriety, and Perspective: An Interpretation and Application of Key Terms in Kenneth Burke's Permanence and Change." *Western Journal of Speech Communication* 53, no. 4 (1989): 327–41.

Rowland, Dunbar. *Jefferson Davis's Place in History As Revealed In His Letters, Papers, and Speeches*. Jackson, MS: Torgerson Press, 1923.

Raleigh (NC) Semi-Weekly Standard. "Confederate Congress," 1863.

Sipiora, Phillip, and James S Baumlin. *Rhetoric and Kairos*. Albany: State University of New York Press, 2002.

Thomas, Emory M, Lesley J Gordon, and John C Inscoe. *Inside The Confederate Nation*. Baton Rouge: Louisiana State University Press, 2005.

Thomas, Emory M. *The Confederate Nation, 1861–1865*. New York: Harper & Row, 1979.

———. *The Confederacy as a Revolutionary Experience*. 2nd ed. Columbia: University of South Carolina, 1991.

Vandiver, Frank Everson. *Jefferson Davis and the Confederate State*. Oxford, UK: Clarendon Press, 1964.

Vico, Giambattista, Giorgio A. Pinton, and Arthur W Shippee. *The Art of Rhetoric*. Amsterdam: Rodopi, 1996.

Western Democrat. "Speech of President Davis to the Legislature of Mississippi, Dec. 26," 1863.

Wills, Garry. *Lincoln at Gettysburg*. New York: Simon & Schuster, 1992.

Wilson, Edmund. *Patriotic Gore*. New York: Oxford University Press, 1962.

Wilson, Kirt H. "The Paradox of Lincoln's Rhetorical Leadership". *Rhetoric & Public Affairs* 3, no. 1 (2000): 15–32.

Wood, Gordon S. *The Creation of the American Republic, 1776–1787*. Chapel Hill: Published for the Institute of Early American History and Culture at Williamsburg, VA, by the University of North Carolina Press, 1969.

———. *The Radicalism of the American Revolution*. New York: A. A. Knopf, 1992.

Woodworth, Steven E. *Jefferson Davis and His Generals*. Lawrence: University Press of Kansas, 1990.

Zarefksy, David. "Consistency and Change in Lincoln's Rhetoric About Equality." *Rhetoric & Public Affairs, no.* 1 (1998): 21–44.

Index